PLEASE DON´T KILL ME MOMMY!

Miguel Angel Kircos

ACKNOWLEDGMENTS

I give thanks to God for having trusted me with the task of preparing such an important material for the purpose of enlightening and bringing truth to many.

I am grateful to the Holy Spirit for His guidance throughout this entire process that culminated in the work you now hold in your hands. When I disposed myself to obey the Lord, His guidance was amazing. The flow of information and help I received was overwhelming.

Many thanks to my beloved wife, Ana Maria, to my sons Sergio, Miguel, Claudia, Marcelo, Eugenia and Pablo. Thanks also to my brethren in the ministry for their collaborative efforts and support.

My thanks to Ricardo Kircos and his wife, Patricia, who have always showed us their support. Many thanks to Lucy Kircos. My thanks to my brethren, Ricardo Ceriani, Tony and Agop Bedikian and their families. To Rolando, Ruben Manoukian and so many other friends whom we love profoundly.

Many thanks to Pastors Alex and Gina Gonzalez, Edgardo and Sonia Surenian, Pablo and Graciela Lago, Claudio y Betty Freidzon, Sergio Enriquez Oliva, Guillermo Di Giovanna, Ruben Alberto and Flavia Gonzalez, Francisco Hernández, Freddy and Alina Muñoz, and Edwin Cardona, who are dear friends and militants in the ministry.

My thanks to Dr. Eduardo Bedrossian and so many others who, if acknowledged, would fill the pages of this book. I am grateful to Roberto Kavlakian, Pablo Tigani, Carlos Contreras, Polo and Estrellita.

My thanks to all the intercessors and all those who support the ministry through their offerings.

Finally, I am grateful to Patricia Gristo for her great help and hard work in this ministry

MIGUEL ÁNGEL KIRCOS

FOREWORD

Every time I hold a baby in my arms for the purpose of dedicating it to the Lord, together with its parents, I give thanks to the Creator of life for a new human being who is afforded an opportunity to live.

As I read this book on abortion, I reflect on the thousands who were never able to see the light of day, nor had the opportunity to be caressed by their mother, or held in the strong arms of their father.

What pain, what sadness, what shame it is to see how low humanity has fallen! They do not only hate, mistreat and kill each other; they've made defenseless creatures, who in their mother's womb, are liken in purity to their Creator, victims of their wickedness.

The author tells us this is not something new, it goes back to Job's time. Yet, it is a reality that at a time of technological and scientific advances and pop culture we have lost sight of the privilege that God has given us: the ability to beget and develop sound, steadfast families, who are filled with love and respect for life.

Every time a baby is aborted, no matter which method is used, the life of a future President of a nation, an exceptional sportsman or woman, an outstanding scientist, an anointed preacher, a self-sacrificing mother, a providing father, and model son or daughter in the midst of a confused generation lost in drugs, alcohol and perverted sex, is cut short.

There have been more deaths resulting from abortion (40,000) in the last thirty years, than from all the wars of the last century together. However, the burden of federal and state laws is on seeking the guilty of great corporate frauds, terrible terrorist acts, mafia crimes and other punishable offenses. They are not realizing abortion is a profitable business for clinics, labs and medical-related entities.

Relevant authorities overlook and ignore it, while continuing to pass laws in favor of abortion, pleading "the right to choose."

As pastor of a Christian church, husband, father and grandfather, I am startled to see how we have transformed the liberty we enjoy from God into uncontrolled freedom that has affected and continues to affect each new generation.

It is my hope and prayer this book will influence those who read it in a positive way; clear up misconceptions and uncover the fact that abortion is a crime; serve as an aid to stop any desire or intention to execute it in the near or distant future.

Pablo Lago

Pastor

La Roca Firme (The Steady Rock)

Christian Fellowship

Hialeah, Florida

COMMENTS ABOUT THE BOOK

You will not be able to read this book and remain indifferent.

Evangelist Miguel Angel Kircos, whom I respect and have known for quite some time, addresses the difficult issue of Abortion with depth and knowledge. From its pages, this book stirs, mobilizes and calls us to reflect on the precious value of life. Even those who failed in this area and suffer because of it will receive God's consolation and mercy by reading its pages.

I applaud its publication and sincerely recommend it.

Claudio J. Freidzon

Pastor

Buenos Aires, Argentina

"Rey de Reyes ("King of Kings") Church

Life is a sacred gift. God, in His sovereignty, is responsible for deciding when human existence should begin and when it should end.

Assaulting human life is contrary to the purposes of our Creator. Regrettably, in these post-modern times, absolute values are no longer revered and certain undeniable and eternal truths are not considered important.

Certainly, man has been created in the image and likeness of God. Every human being is unique and irreplaceable. This is why abortion is not only a crime, although some "progressive" legislatures allow it, but it's worse than that: it is a sin of terrible consequences.

I praise the publication of this work authored by Miguel Angel Kircos and I am certain it will be a worthy contribution to all those who read it.

Dr. Ricardo M. Bedrossian

Pastor

Cristo es el Cambio ("Christ brings Change")
Church

In an unadorned style, using real-life examples of every day life, some of them hair-raising, Evangelist Miguel Ang Kircos, travels through all the roads leading to abortion. He points out, in no uncertain terms, to the existence of lie inside a mother's womb. Adding to it, are plain and simple concepts as evidence of God's pre-conceived plans for every human being He creates.

This book will help understand why a seeming solution such as abortion contradicts God's will. The author also offers a way out for those who, due to lack of knowledge or by mistake, underwent an abortion or accompanied someone in that experience.

Miguel Ángel Kircos is truly one of those persons who are inspired by God to address this and other complex issues. His testimony and dedication to the

Lord endorse his writings. This book will edify those versed on the subject matter, while delivering a clear warning to those unaware of the consequences stemming from such a decision.

I believe the reading of this book is a must for those who have gone through an abortion or believe abortion is not a crime. For those who, after acknowledging the significance of this mistake, feel discouraged, this book will give you a way out, a word of hope through God's forgiveness and consolation

Pablo Tigani

Índice

A LETTER FROM AN ABORTED BABY TO ITS MOTHER

Dear Mommy:

Remember me? I'm your baby. You didn't manage to get rid of me forever. God gave me an eternal soul the instant I was conceived. I never saw the light of day, but I live forever.

I know why you killed me. You were ashamed of me. You didn't want to be an unwed mother. I was the result of an affair. You were too young to have me. Your parents would never forgive you. What would your friends say? And so on and so on.

I will never forget the time you carried me in your womb, I felt so low. I understand that you didn't want me; after all, what would those around you think? You had to eliminate the mistake by getting rid of the evidence, and that was I.

I don't condone your crime, but I forgive you. I forgive Daddy for being so irresponsible as to abandon us. I also forgive the doctor that stained his hands with my innocent blood. And the nurse who helped him.

It was painful when he punctured me with that huge needle and then tore me to bits in cold blood! I know you will never forget the unique noise of that vacuum that sucked up my tiny broken body.

I know that it was a traumatic experience for you, and that you now bear the secret in silence trying to convince yourself that it was nothing. It was something. It was someone. It was me, your baby.

I'm aware Mommy, of your long restless nights. I know you struggled with your decision to abort me. I know you still dream about me, and more than once you have regretfully asked yourself if I were a boy or a girl. You have wondered how it might have been were I still alive and how much joy I would have brought to you...

I look like you. How can you forget me? I constantly to God our Father that He takes away the nightmares that disturb your sleep so much and have you in a living hell! And so, I recommend that you make your peace with the Author of life.

Dear Mommy, I want you to be happy. And you know what? Only Christ can heal your wounds, even those you inflicted on yourself when you aborted me.

As I write, I have here besides me a friend. His mother killed him too because she said she was too young to be a mother.

He didn't get a name from his parents either, but he got one from God. He loves us infinitely. I have a lot of friends who met with the same fate. Peter was aborted because his mother was raped. All of the hate and anguish coming from that was poured out on the poor innocent one. He asked himself, "If my mommy was mad at the man who raped her why did she kill me? I would have loved her forever and never been ashamed of her."

Here in the Kingdom of love, we only understand the language of love. For that reason, we don't understand all the "arguments" for abortion: deformed fetus, rape, poor parents, not wanting more children (assuming that the small family lives better), etc.

They tell me that not even the bloody world wars, nor Hitler with his lethal gas chambers, have caused as brutal and cruel massacre. With all the abortions the world has been deprived of brilliant pastors, poets, doctors, musicians, painters and architects.

Don't cry Mommy. Maybe you're wondering where I am. Don't worry; I'm in the arms of Jesus. He loved me enough to shed his blood for me. In Him we all find life.

Let me conclude by asking a favor of you. Not for me, but for other babies. Don't kill them like I was! If you know a young lady who wants an abortion, or someone who argues in favor of abortion, or a doctor that by such murder mocks Hippocrates, or a nurse who participates in the crime, extend to them the love of God, our Father. Then, remember us and tell them not to kill any more. Tell them that children belong to God. Tell them all that we have a right to live just like they do, and that even if no one loves us, we have a right to live and love.

Love,

Your aborted baby

INTRODUCTION

"Please don't kill me Mommy!" is the exclamation of the unborn from the womb of the mother who gave it life. The outcry arises from the realization of the danger that it is facing when the instrument that will bring its death gets close to its small, defenseless body. It expects to receive love and caring, but instead what it gets is hate and cruelty!

"Please don't kill me Mommy!" is the tragic phrase of those babies, still in their mothers' wombs, who unfortunately pay dearly for one of the most serious and horrible problems plaguing humanity. It is a problem whose very name represents one of the worst evils to afflict the world: ABORTION!

I firmly believe that this is one of the most serious matters of all times that humanity has had to face. On the one hand, there are overpopulated countries whose governments want to control the birth rate by implementing absurd and inhuman laws. Any and every means available is used to enforce these laws, the most popular of which is abortion.

On the other hand, there are those countries where modernism and a comfortable lifestyle have become the predominant concern of many, so much so that they have become insensitive to the cry of these little, defenseless creatures whose lives are torn from them in silence. They are not given the opportunity to live according to what God, the creator of this world, has established. For many, the arrival of these little ones is an inconvenience that they didn't ask for, a burden that might limit their licentiousness in some way.

I must confess that, for as long as I can remember, I had heard these words through several sources, but, like a lot of folks, was indifferent to their meaning. I have mentioned in preaching on occasion, but never gave them the attention they deserve until God pierced my heart with them.

The widespread indifference that abounds, even in Christian circles, in the face of such wholesale slaughter is indeed painful. As a general rule, we can grasp the magnitude of this monstrosity when it hits close to home, as when a neighbor, or a family member, or even our own daughter commits such a dastardly murder.

I am writing today with a heart that has been wounded by the loss of millions of innocent lives. My purpose is to alert those who are faced with the decision of whether to let live the child that a mother is carrying in her womb or to prevent it from seeing the light of day.

My hope is that the Holy Spirit might use this book to touch the lives of many of the women who think that abortion is a solution. I also hope that they might be persuaded to let their child be born and thus enjoy raising them in the love and the fear of the Lord.

CHAPTER 1

AN UNEXPECTED MESSAGE AND THE RESULT OF OBEDIENCE

I rarely mentioned the term abortion in my evangelistic work over the years. When I did, it was usually just a passing reference in a list of sins that plague mankind today. Then, on one of those occasions the term seemed to jump out at me. It took on a new meaning for me and so overwhelmed me that I came face to face with the tragedy of human suffering. I must confess that the idea filled me with anguish.

My turning point came when I was getting ready to preach to a crowd that had gathered in Villa Hayes, Paraguay. The message was already prepared. Everything was set. But before going out on the platform that night, I was praying and asking God to work in a special way. Suddenly, I heard a voice inside of me that said, "Tonight, I want you to preach on abortion!"

It was difficult for me to accept such a request, because I thought it would be impossible to preach for forty minutes on the subject. I had never done that before and besides, it didn't fit with my style.

But I didn't want to be like Jonah, the prophet of old, whom God instructed to go to Nineveh for forty days to warn them of the wrath of God that would befall them because of their evil ways, giving them time to repent and avoid their punishment.

It was a great challenge for Jonah. At first he fled, but then repented and obeyed God's command. The whole city repented, from the King on down to the rank and file. God forgave them and didn't destroy the city.

God used this biblical story to refresh my mind and help me grasp what it was He wanted me to do.

I felt that the Lord wanted me to speak on abortion, even though I had not prepared anything on the subject. It was a time of inner struggle, doubt, and searching for ideas, but finally I realized that the only decision I could make was to obey the voice of the Lord.

WHEN WE OBEY, GOD BLESSES US

And so I understood that if God were asking it of me, He would give me the appropriate words to say.

When it came time for me to preach, in obedience I opened my mouth and for twenty minutes -nearly the first half of the sermon- I spoke about abortion. I don't remember now the exact words I spoke, but I do remember the impression it made on a woman when I issued the altar call and called people to settle their accounts with God, as the only way to achieve peace and happiness. The woman came running to the altar under deep conviction; and with her eyes brimming with tears, she knelt down and begged for divine forgiveness.

When the meeting was over, she approached me with her husband and little girl, thanking me for the message I had preached. She admitted to me that the next morning she had an appointment at a clinic to get an abortion. It was wonderful to have obeyed the voice of

God. Among the lives that were saved that night was a defenseless creature, who though destined to die without seeing the light of day, was given a new hope of living through the obedience and faith of its mother.

That day when I returned home my heart had been stirred, but I was also very happy. God had abundantly blessed me, due to my obedience and the obedience of a couple who reversed the horrible decision they had made.

That occasion marked the beginning of a burden that has resulted in the book you now hold in your hands. My return home that day wasn't the same as before. On the way home, the Holy Spirit reminded me of how Moses' little sister must have felt when she saw that her attempts to save the life of her newborn brother were successful. I even remembered the miraculous escape of our Lord from the murderous abortion attempts of Herod. Just knowing that the woman that night would spare the life of her baby flooded my mind with all sorts of examples.

That event awakened in me the reality of this abominable act that plagues humanity. From that moment on, I have had a burden for the number of these cases that happen, even in the bosom of our churches. How many homes suffer from the malignant scourge of abortion?

All of that happened, simply because I obeyed the voice of God and did what He asked. **We must obey that still, divine voice.**

Just as God spoke to me when I was about to start my evangelistic message, I am sure that there is an inner voice that comes to every woman who considers abortion, trying to stop her from becoming the murderer of her own flesh and blood. That voice that prompts a woman to debate between two options, to get an abortion or to let the baby live, is the voice of God.

He doesn't want anyone to perish, and so He still speaks to sinners. That voice creates restlessness during the nights leading up to the moment of carrying out the macabre deed. The creation of life is something so divine that the Psalmist David praises His creator by saying, "Your hand made me and formed me" (Psalm 119:73), and again, "For you created my inmost being; you knit me together in my mother's womb" (Psalm 139:13).

What I am trying to say with this is that, even when two unbelievers get together and conceive a new life, though they may not recognize Christ as Savior, though they may be the most miserable of sinners, the mere act of conceiving a human life takes the intervention of God. How then can we put the decision to take a life in the hands of a mere human being and take it away from God, who created life itself?

I know of cases where that small voice -which we will call the "voice of God"- was so insistent that the woman abandoned her idea to abort her child. We must obey that persistent, divine voice. If you obey it, you will be rewarded not only with the child who will be born, but also with all of the blessings that come from obedience to God.

If you disobey that voice, the days following the crime will be bitter. The nightmare will never fade. You will never do completely satisfied.

I know people who after an abortion have gone on to have more children than they should in hopes of covering up their guilty conscience. They think that in this way they can put behind them the crime committed, but they will never be able to forget that little defenseless one they deprived of life.

That is why it is important to obey the voice of God. The main reason for this book is to raise awareness of the fact that abortion is a tragic and diabolical act.

CHAPTER 2

WHAT IS ABORTION?

In order to understand what abortion represents, we must have an awareness of its significance and purpose.

Abortion is the decision to eliminate or get rid of something in process that was created with a purpose.

For example, sometimes NASA will build a space ship with a particular purpose in mind, yet at a given moment in the process, whether it is in the manufacture or in the launch phase, they decide to abort the mission. That means that they have decided to eliminate or discontinue it. Just so, some of the projects or missions that are born in the heart of man are eliminated by his own choice, whether that be good or evil.

Likewise, when a person decides to abort the child who is being formed in her womb, it means to:

Decide - Eliminate - Undo

Abortion is the halting of the development of the fetus in its mother's womb. It is important to point out that there are spontaneous abortions that are not induced because of a decision on the part of the parents, but that come about because of complications from the pregnancy. In that case, the fetus is aborted in a natural way that is not induced. When that happens, there is no transgression of the laws of God or the laws of man.

On the other hand, when a couple and their doctor decide on an abortion, there is always a premeditation and resolve on the part of a human being.

There is a big difference between a spontaneous abortion and an induced abortion. Abortion, or feticide, is the elimination or murder of a child in the womb of its at any point in its development, from fertilization (when the sperm and the egg come together) until the moment just prior to birth. It is a transgression of the fifth of the Ten Commandments: "Thou shalt not kill".

Human life starts at conception. At that instant, God creates a unique eternal soul that is made in the image of God. It is God who forms and molds it with His own hands, mother and watches over it while it is still a small, shapeless embryo (see Psalm 139:13). Even while it is still in the womb - as many Biblical texts point out- man is the highest creation of a loving Father.

Those who defend and promote abortion always want to cover up the criminal nature of this shameful deed with the use of confusing or evasive terminology, hiding the murder behind expressions such as "voluntary termination of pregnancy" or such concepts as "pro-choice" or "right of reproductive health." None of these linguistic stunts however, can hide the fact that abortion is **murder.**

WHY IS ABORTION MURDER?

The use of the word "fetus" can lead people to think that what is in the womb is not really a baby. In fact, there are those who consider it simply something along the lines of deformed tissue... However, at the moment of conception there is already an independent life within the body of the mother. It is a soul, a human being, which is beginning its growth process.

During the pregnancy, the baby hears everything and after just a few months of development even recognizes its mother and father's voices, responds to auditory and luminescent stimuli, as can be verified by certain fetal health evaluation and well-being methods.

I can affirm this by personal experience. When our daughter, Claudia, was expecting her first baby, she and her husband, Marcelo, spoke, sang and stroked the baby through its mother's belly. They asked God that when the baby saw the light of this world, He would form his character, the features of his body, etc. I can attest to the fact that Andrew -who is ten years old already- is a living example today of today of the prayer of his parents and of what they communicated to him during the pregnancy.

REASONS FOR ABORTION

Following conception, some people are so overcome with a number of fears that they opt for an abortion. If the couple in question is a married couple, they may not want to have a baby at present for fear that their economic situation may not allow them to provide adequately for the child, or because they have had a previous bad experience with another child, or know about a bad experience of another couple who ended up in divorce, or because of the risks that can arise during the pregnancy or at the moment of birth. Then because of these fears, or maybe some other fear that hasn't been mentioned, they decide to seek an abortion.

Let me say to these couples that rejecting what God gives to us is a sin. But I would like to add that if God sends a child into the world, whether it be by His decision or by what might be considered an accidental pregnancy, God will always provide the sustenance needed for its development in all areas of its life, such as: food, education, and care. Also, we should never forget about the sovereignty of God, who has promised a guardian angel for every child in this world.

Certainly, risks always exist and can come, but I assure you that it is worthwhile to take the risks, because a child can be one of God's richest sources of blessing.

After a year of marriage, my wife, Ana Maria and I had two wonderful twin boys. But they both were born prematurely and died within a few hours. The pain, the confusion, the fears and the disappointments overwhelmed our feelings. You can imagine what we went through. Yet, with our trust in God, a year later came our oldest boy, Sergio, then Claudia, Miguel and finally, Pablo.

Today, some of them are married, and the others will be soon. We have two grandchildren who enrich our lives even when we go through storms and hard times.

In the case of unmarried couples who live together, a child would be for them a seal of their carnal and spiritual union, even though it is not approved by God. They might seek an abortion because they think that there would be less chance of going their separate ways if things didn't work out for them, that they might have to face hard circumstances or simply because they don't wish to assume a formal commitment for life.

To these couples I would say that the absence of a marriage commitment doesn't afford any liberty, nor security and much less true love; but rather a superficial and selfish love coupled with fear and doubts about the future.

Actually, living together doesn't free one from the bonds of matrimony, for the Word of God teaches in Genesis 2:24 that a man should leave his father and his mother and be joined to his wife, and the two shall become one flesh.

That indicates that when a man and a woman start living together and solidify their relationship with sexual intercourse, they are already joined, they are one, just as in marriage. So my advice is that they should legally marry and if through the laws of nature God gives you a precious child, don't add the horror of destroying it to the mistakes of living together.

The case might also be that when the woman is pregnant the father doesn't feel that the pregnancy should continue. If the mother wishes to let the child be born, but the father opposes it, and persists in that position, before running the risk of alienating the father, the woman gives in to the pressure and decides to seek an abortion.

My advice to that mother is that she should stand firm until the bitter end. Even if the father abandons her.

God in His love and justice will not abandon her. God will take care of her and the baby and will help to supply all of their needs, because it is right before God to defend the life that you are carrying.

At any rate, it is better to loose someone who is insensitive to the love and fear of God, even if he once was the love of your life, than to kill your child.

Psalm 27:10 (NIV - New International Version) says:

"Though my father and mother forsake me, the LORD will receive me".

Actually, many countries have homes that offer help to single mothers or women unable to support themselves spiritually or financially; so before seeking an abortion it is worth looking into these institutions.

There are cases in which a man and a woman give in to the sexual temptations of the moment and fall into the sin of adultery or fornication, and the woman ends up pregnant. There are a number of reasons that may make them want to seek an abortion. One of them might be that he, or she, or maybe both are single, and a child, as in some of the previous cases I mentioned, would place them in a compromising situation. Added to that would be the shame of being found out and living life with the stain of the sin.

On this point let me say that abortion is not the solution to cover the stain of sin or to undo the compromising situation. Rather, it is confession, repentance and the bravery to face the problem and solve it. It doesn't make sense to add another sin to the previous one.

What we need to understand here is that the sin was committed at the moment of the illicit sexual encounter.

A baby, under such circumstances, tends to imply a change of plans and a sense of shame for the family. Speaking to this let me say that God will never allow those who act in righteousness and truth to be shamed. You can be sure then that those who would mock or slander you will have to face the judgment of God.

In the case of a prostitute, a pregnancy would be a burden that would limit her freedom to continue practicing her trade. Also, the idea of social prejudice and the child being labeled as "the child of a prostitute" may prompt her to seek an abortion. The Bible mentions cases of abortion (see Exodus 21:22-23). If an involuntary abortion was condemned, how much more an intentional one! Job also spoke of the matter, which would indicate that this was something that even happened in his day. Maybe women such as Mary Magdalene and others who followed Jesus committed this terrible sin, which in the eyes of God is considered like any other sin, yet God's grace was sufficient for them.

Another argument from liberal, feminist, or pro-abortion groups is that women should have the right to decide if want the child within them to be born or not. They think that with abortion an unwanted child can be avoided or one that wouldn't be loved and given the nurture necessary for them to live a decent life. For these groups, abortion is a way to free a woman from something that would tie her down or limit her freedom. They assume that abortion the means to correct the mistake of irresponsibility, negligence, accident or ignorance that results from a simple sexual encounter.

Behind all of this is the idea that abortion should be a valid way to correct a situation that if left to continue unchanged would have an undesired or unforeseen result. Yet, what is worse is that abortion is a greater crime that is committed to cover up, in many cases, embarrassing acts and situations recognized as sin, such as lust, infidelity and unbridled sex. In other words, loose and indiscriminate sexual intercourse outside of marriage.

ESSENTIALLY, THE DECISION TO ABORT IS A MATTER OF COMMITTING ONE CRIME TO COVER UP ANOTHER.

It is definitively impossible to cover up one sin with another. When we understand that extramarital sex is a transgression of the law of God, then abstinence can help us avoid another transgression that is just as cruel - that of abortion.

CHAPTER 3

ABORTION: CRIME OR RIGHT

Toward the end of September 2000, the U.S. Food and Drug Administration (FDA) approved the sale to the public of the RU 486 pill to be used to terminate pregnancies within the first 50 days. Women, then, if they decide to do so, can easily terminate a pregnancy themselves with this pill without having to see a doctor.

Once the FDA announced publicly their approval for the sale of the pill, as well as the restrictions for its use, the abortion debate was re-ignited. Liberal and feminist groups immediately applauded the decision, because this –they claimed - is a positive step in the direction of recognizing the right of women to choose what affects their own bodies.

On the other hand, religious leaders from various levels and denominations opposed to abortion raised their voices to condemn the approval of the drug, because with its use -they affirmed- green light was given to indiscriminately eliminate defenseless creatures.

In certain parts of the world, such as in most Latin American countries, abortion is banned by law, though there are exceptions to cover the cases of pregnancy resulting from rape to a mentally retarded woman. Yet, in spite of the ban, several health organizations indicate that the practice of abortion is a widespread and daily occurrence that is done in secret with unscientific instruments or methods.

In Argentina, due basically to its secrecy, the actual number of abortions is unknown, but, based on the number of women who come to be seen for complications resulting from the procedure, it is estimated that the number exceeds 500,000 a year. This statistic came from Argentina's own minister of health, who also mentioned that the annie births in the country are 700,000. Regrettably, this officer believes that it would be good to legalize abortion in an effort to avoid the 500,000 annual deaths that occur in underground clinics, while forgetting about the 500,000 who are not allowed to live.

In the United States the data is more specific because abortions are performed in authorized abortion clinics. A conservative figure is upwards of 1.500.000 per year.

These cases run greater risks because the fetus is killed and the mother can later die from a serious infection or hemorrhage.

This is one of the most compelling reasons, according to the feminist groups and others who defend the right of women to seek an abortion, because once it is legalized the mortality rate of women from abortion will decrease and competent medical attention will be available. But if we agree with this argument, certainly the pro-choice organizations will keep on raising their voices and the confusion will continue.

ABORTION AND TEENS

Behind all of this, is a great marketing strategy to manipulate public opinion, especially targeted to young people.

When the famous RU 486 pill made its appearance a decade ago, the French government at that time gave in to pressure from the feminist groups to legalize abortion. But the years since then have shown that the move was not an effective one since now it is the teens who come to the clinics for abortions. The amazing thing is that many of them come accompanied by their mothers.

The high demand has these clinics overextended thus making the girls travel to other countries where the crime is legal. Some of the girls, who don't have the economic resources to travel, end up committing suicide.

In the United States, the Clinton administration, copying the French model, undertook-during its sad and immoral presidential term - a number of measures to legalize the practice of abortion. For many teens, the sexual revolution starts around the age of 13, but can also occur in some girls as young as 10.

This sexual revolution or carnal freedom at such a young age is a reflection of a bankrupt and decadent society in which there is no strong family circle or identity. What there is an obsession with making money to be able to dress in the latest fashion and seduce those of the opposite sex, or, in some cases, those of the same sex.

In this wild and dissipated lifestyle, when these young girls get pregnant, they mistakenly think that abortion is the ideal means of avoiding the guilt and the responsibility for a failed love affair or simply a youthful fling. That is what lies behind abortion, which becomes the means for covering up a multitude of sins that are committed since the youth.

By promoting these measures, the big drug companies are making millions of dollars off of the sexual escapades of the youth, millions of dollars that are multiplied even more with the sale of the famous pill Mifeprex, which is the trade name of RU 486.

There is no doubt that a public conscience ceases to exist and life takes on a lesser value when business is at stake, for earning money at the expense of the murder of babies is the most loathsome profession that can be undertaken.

In the next chapter, we will look at a few testimonies of women, mainly young people or teens, who have gone through the experience of an abortion.

CHAPTER 4

THE BIBLE, ABORTION AND THE ANTICHRIST

Although many people say the Bible doesn't refer to abortion as such, as it is the case with other established doctrines of the Christian Faith -such as the Trinity-, there are references that relate to it. The prophet Amos condemns the Ammonites for practicing abortion with the following words,

This is what the Lord says, 'For three sins of Ammon, even for four, I will not turn back my wrath. Because he ripped open the pregnant women of Gilead.' (Amos 1:13)

Though the crime committed is not specifically named, what was done is perfectly clear.

We can affirm that abortion is anti-Christian for the following reasons:

1. The Bible tells us that when God created man He breathed into his nostrils the breath of life (see Genesis 2:7). The breath of life is life itself, and that comes from God.

2. Also, the Bible teaches that from the beginning, Christ (the Word) is the one who gives life, because in Him there is life and all life was made through Him (see John 1:4).

In the same Gospel (5:21), it says that Jesus is the one who gives life. Christ came to give physical life to all those who are conceived in their mother's wombs and eternal life to those who repent of their sins. In short, we can say that Christ's intention is always to give life.

On the other hand, there is someone who has come to kill, and that is who the Bible presents as the antichrist.

The antichrist is anyone who rebels against Christ and is opposed to everything that He does and stands for. That is to say that, everyone who opposes the right to life and who uses any method to kill is the antichrist.

Jesus himself said that the enemy comes to rob, kill and destroy. Anyone who destroys a life is the antichrist, and will be judged as such.

Doctors who perform abortions, as well as the parents who seek an abortion, are the antichrist. The only exception would be the abortions that occur naturally.

The antichrist is a spirit that opposes life. It rejects everything that comes from Christ, and many people under its influence become instruments of death and destruction.

CHAPTER 5

TESTIMONIES

A Brazilian girl

Two months ago I went through the most painful experience of my life. My boyfriend was from the town of Curitiba (Brazil) and I lived in San Pablo. We didn't see each other much, but loved each other passionately and in a crazy passionate moment, I ended up pregnant. We had been together for eight months. He was four years younger than me and my mother argued a lot with him. I had a lot of misgivings as to what to do. Time passed until I decided to have an abortion. I was already nearly four months pregnant. We were an unmarried couple living together, but my boyfriend just wasn't the same.

Then I went to Curitiba. He had purchased some pills called Cytotec. I took the pills in an act of desperation. Four hours later I was in the hospital with bleeding and acute pain. They gave me a wheel chair because I couldn't even walk. I went to the bathroom, and couldn't help but to look into the toilet bowl. It was then that I experienced an emotional crisis: it **was a boy**. The hands, the legs, the ears, all perfectly formed... I cried a lot. When the nurse came to flush the toilet, I started to despair. I wanted to put my baby back inside of me. Remorse overwhelmed me immediately, but regrettably, it was too late.

The next day I went in for follow-up treatment. My boyfriend went with me; but even so I felt alone... We hugged each other and I went in to surgery and waited for the anesthesiologist to come. At that moment I heard the cry of a baby.

I was recovering from the anesthesia together with other women who had given birth, when a nurse came by with a baby in her arms. She asked me if I wanted to see it. At that moment I felt a great sense of grief in my heart. How I wished that boy was mine! Today, he would be with me.

I broke up with my boyfriend and never spoke to him again. I know that he was mentally distraught over what happened I needed him to support me, and I just didn't get it.

Every night I ask God to protect my son, wherever he may be. Also I ask my son to forgive me and assure him that all I wish to do is bring him back.

Name withheld. November 24, 2000

What impresses me the most about this story of abortion and its fallout is the fact that, upon seeing her baby boy the toilet bowl, this young girl not only experienced an immediate remorse, but has the enduring desire to bring her boy back to life. We know that that is physically impossible. But this testimony, though heartbreaking makes it clear that before seeking an abortion the spiritual sentimental and physical consequences should be weighed. The couple broke up, yet even so they both were left with the burden of grief for the abortion of their son.

Another Brazilian Student

I arrived at the clinic with my boyfriend and my mother. I thought it would be easy. The doctor explained to me how the modern and safe American abortion by suction technology worked. It would only take a maximum of five minutes.

I had been pregnant for two months. It was to be fast and simple. A shot in the arm put me to sleep, but not completely I could feel what the doctor was doing inside of me as if it were a dream. It didn't take long. They put me in a recovery room and I was asleep there for another ten minutes. Then I got dressed and went out to meet my mother and my boyfriend. There I threw up.

The whole thing took about a half hour, we left there and headed for McDonald's. I felt happy and relieved. From there I went straight to work. At that time I was teaching English classes. I was substituting for a colleague who was pregnant and about to give birth to her baby.

It was then, upon my return, that I started to notice babies. All of them were so pure and innocent; the most angelical creatures in the world... I suffered a lot, too much. I still suffer. I didn't have anyone to talk to; no one I could share my experience with, especially my guilt. At home, abortion was never talked about, it was a forbidden subject. I went through torture with my boyfriend. I wanted to talk. He could tell that I had regretted having the abortion. We continued to live together for three years after the incident.

Today, my boy would have been two and a half years old. His name would have been Angel. I promised myself one thing I would never have another abortion. Neither would I get pregnant unless I was absolutely prepared. The memories are so real, and now I feel guilty.

I write these lines in honor of my baby on November 2, 1999.

Name withheld.

The remorse and the burden of guilt is what tortures one. Even when an abortion is successful, the inevitable end result is a sense of guilt that turns happiness and freedom in a terrible bondage which then becomes a curse.

A Spontaneous Abortion

It was an unexpected pregnancy. At first I was happy, but then despair set in. How would the father take the news of the baby? He found out about it the same day that I did and asked me to terminate the pregnancy. It was the hardest decision of my life, but I determined to have the child, with or without him. Little by little he came to accept it, but reluctantly and even with some indifference.

I would talk to the baby and explain to him that given time his father would learn to love him.

I had to rest in bed for fourteen weeks due to a hemorrhage that lasted for ten days. After that we went to the coast. One night I was in a lot of pain and my water broke. I was losing my son. There was heavy bleeding. We were facing a hopeless situation.

I asked God to let the agony be over soon and not let the baby suffer.

We return to Victoria, were my doctor was waiting to care for me. That was barely a week ago. Now I am trying to overcome the guilt. I feel guilty for not being able to do anything. The grief is considerable, but the comfort can be greater.

Son: you have gone, but you are very much loved. Every night I hear you singing in my dreams and I imagine you smiling for me. Your memory is tucked away in our hearts. Forgive me son.

The love of a mother

Flavia Jazmin

flaviayazmin@yahoo.com

3/8/2000

In spite of it not having been an induced abortion, there is still a sense of guilt, grief and sadness. That is how I feel along with my wife, Ana Maria, when our twins died. Even though they were born naturally, there was a feeling of guilt and grief. In this young lady's case, she blamed herself for not being able to do anything. In our case, we blamed ourselves for possible negligence.

It is important to know that God is always willing to forgive and comfort us, but also it is necessary for us to forgive ourselves. Many times we accept God's forgiveness, but continue to torture ourselves because we have not forgiven ourselves.

Brenda Pratt Shafer, nurse, September 1993

Brenda P. Shafer, a nurse with thirteen years of experience, was sent by the health organization that she worked for to assist in an abortion clinic. As she considered herself to be pro-abortion, she didn't imagine that the work would create major problems for her. She was wrong.

This is her story:

I stood beside the doctor to assist him in an abortion that he was performing on a woman who was two-months pregnant.

The baby's heartbeats could clearly be seen on the ultrasound screen. The doctor extracted the baby's whole body, except for the tiny head. The baby's body was wreathing, its small fingers opening and closing. He was kicking his feet in despair. The doctor took an instrument and squeezed the back of the baby's head, and in a panic reaction it opened its arms as if it wanted to avoid what was happening, just as a baby would react if it were about to fall.

Then the doctor opened the instrument and inserted the suction tube in the hole to suck out the baby's brain. At that point it was totally dead.

I never returned to that clinic. The face of that baby still haunts me. It was a perfect little face, the most angelic face I had ever seen.

Believe me that if the electric chair were the punishment for those who murder babies, there would not be enough chairs in the world.

But I know that one day there will be a trial in which He who sits on the throne will condemn them to an eternal torment. They can only escape it if they repent and discontinue these incredibly destructive practices.

Assistant to Dr. David Brewer

I remember when the incision for a cesarean was made before the doctor broke the water, we could see the baby rocking in the amniotic sack.

The thought came to me: "My God, it's a person!" When he broke the water, I felt a horrible pain in my heart. He performed the birth of the baby and I couldn't even touch it.

I consider myself a good assistant. I simply watched what was happening. Eventually, what had happened started to penetrate my calloused heart and mind. We had just taken a small baby - who made low noises, moved around and played - and we put it in a stainless steel jar.

Every time I would return, while we were sewing up the incision in the uterus, I could see the baby playing and rocking itself in that jar. As time went on, he rocked and played less.

Later, when the surgery was over, I remember returning to look at the fetus, which was still alive. I could see the chest rise as it was trying to breathe in some air and its heart was beating.

A defenseless creature, even when it is removed from its mother's abdomen, fights for its existence until the time established by God. Of course, man is more interested in the profits to be made than the life of this small creature left to die in a cold stainless jar, who struggles for its life up to its last breath.

A defenseless creature, even when it is removed from it mother's abdomen, fights for its existence until the time established by God. Of course, man is more interested in the profits to be made than the life of this small creature left to die in a cold stainless steel jar, who struggles for its life up to its last breath.

Another Testimony

I went into an abortion clinic in Washington, DC on April 6, 1988. Right away they gave me a valium to settle me down and probably to keep me from backing out.

They charged me $750 and I was committed. In the waiting room were at least twenty other women. One of them, who was eight months pregnant, said that she had to wait until that time in order to save enough money.

I thought that in my case it was a bit late to have an abortion. I was convinced that what I had carried inside of me for 18 weeks was just tissue.

They had me do a sonogram, but wouldn't let me listen to it. Then I had to undergo a psychological evaluation to ensure that I was able to continue. The evaluation took five minutes, and in spite of the fact that I was crying and experiencing convulsions, they determined that I was able to continue. When they sensed that I wanted to back out, they seemed like salesmen trying to close a deal.

When the moment came, I was not given any anesthesia but was tied to my bed. Then I endured the most terrible and painful experience that I have ever had in my life. I cried out desperately and the nurses were shouting at me to calm down. They said that if I didn't stop moving my colon and uterus would be damaged. I felt blood draining under my hips and the suction was so strong that it seemed that all of my organs were being suctioned out.

When I begged them to stop and asked if it was over, they responded by saying that they had to make sure that all the parts were there.

Parts? I thought that they were just tissue!

All of a sudden, I could see a nurse in front of me with my beautiful baby in pieces. Body parts were spread out on a tray.

They quickly hid the tell tale evidence of the crime and took me to the recovery room. There were other girls there. We were all crying in the fetal position. They sent me home without even showing any intention to observe me to see if everything was fine.

When I was going home on the bus, I bled so much that the blood soaked through my hose and ran down my legs. When I arrived home my parents asked me how it went. I led them to believe that everything was fine and that it was easy.

I fell on my bed and started to cry uncontrollably. I felt sad and empty. I felt horrible!

I have never talked about the abortion since that day and tried to put it out of my mind, but ended up with a post abortion syndrome anyway. I've experienced anguish, depression, remorse and other types of grief that I wouldn't wish on my worst enemy.

May God have mercy on these precious souls.

In memory of my son, Christopher.

12/1/87 - 4/6/88

Montangem Lily writes this very interesting article entitled Aferrarse a la Vida (Clinging to Life) in a neighborhood magazine:

A photographer who was covering the unprecedented medical feat of surgery on a 21-week old fetus still in its mother's womb to correct a problem of spinal bifida, never imagined that his camera would capture what is maybe the most eloquent pro-life argument to date.

As Paul Harris was covering a breakthrough in fetal surgery at Vanderbilt University in Nashville, Tennessee, he captured the moment in which the baby reached out of its mother's uterus with its small arm to grasp the finger of the surgeon that was about to do the operation.

The spectacular picture was run by several newspapers in the United States, and its repercussions were felt throughout the world.

The small hand that captured the world's attention belongs to Samuel Alexander, whose birth was to take place on September 28 of this past year (year not given). On the day that the picture was taken, his mother was barely 5 months pregnant.

When we think about it, it becomes evident that the picture speaks volumes.

The life of the baby was literally hanging from a thread. The specialists knew that they would not be able to keep the baby alive outside of its mother's womb and so would have to operate to correct the fatal defect and then close the uterus so that the baby could continue its normal development.

The image was considered one of the most important medical photos of late and the record of one of the most extraordinary operations in the world.

Samuel became the youngest patient to ever undergo that type of operation, and it is possible that, now outside of his mother's womb, Samuel Alexander reaches his arm out anew to grasp the hand of Dr. Bruner.

Television anchor, Justin McCarthy, said that it is impossible to not be moved by the powerful image of such little hand grasping the finger of the surgeon and makes us think about how a hand can save lives.

Life, the most precious gift, depends on all of us!

The famous picture is published on the Internet.

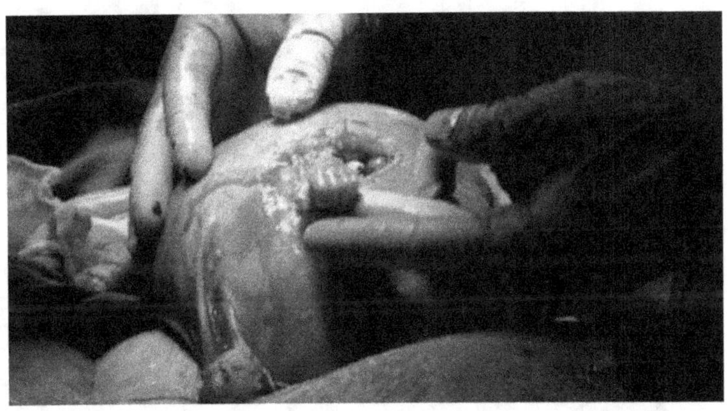

CHAPTER 6

VARIOUS ABORTION METHOD

Let's take a look now at a few images of babies during gestation and pregnancy, and some of the methods used in abortion. All of them are real, and they will help us to understand that what is growing in the womb of the mother is not just a "fetus" but a human being.

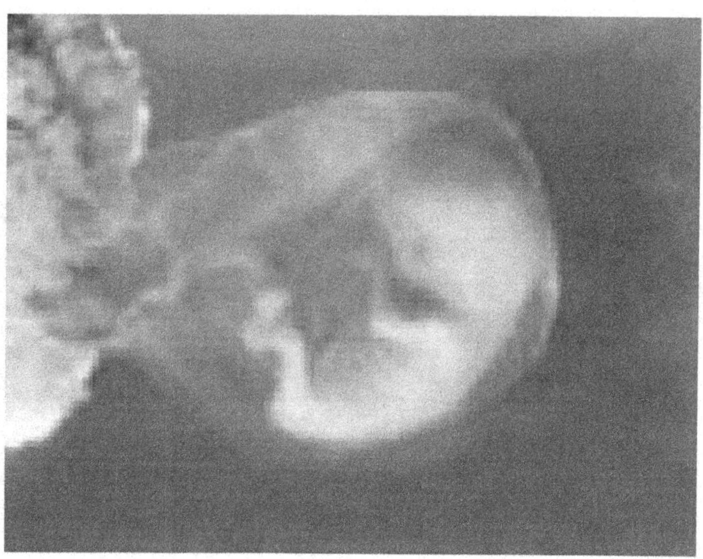

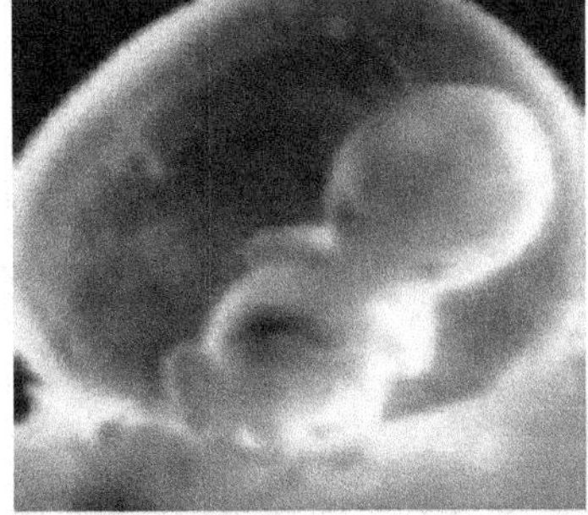

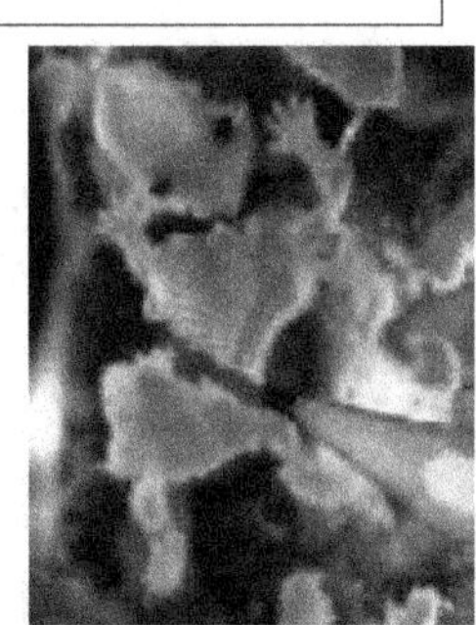

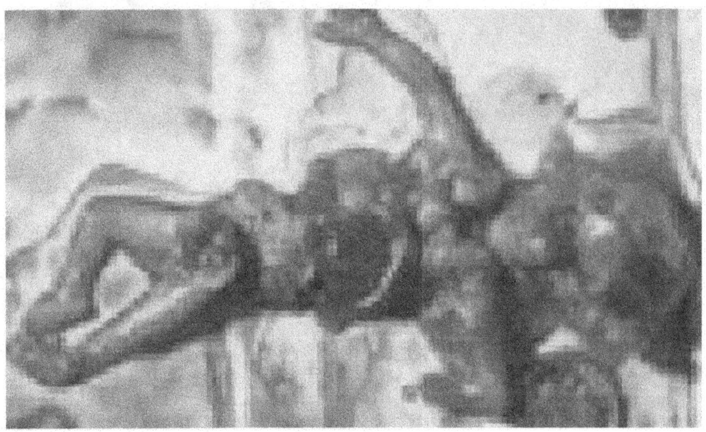

This is an 8 to 10-week old baby

He or she is already grasping with its hands whatever is within its reach. At this point in its development, its heart beat will register on an electrocardiogram and it can be seen swimming in the amniotic fluid.

From this stage on, all the bodily functions of the fetus work on their own: it breathes, it digests food, it swallows, it urinates, etc. The miniature body of the baby is complete. That is apparent when we can see that even his feet are perfect.

The following picture shows an abortion using aspiration or suction.

This was a 10 to 14-week-old fetus. Well formed parts of its little body are evident in the picture. Through the suction method of abortion, the body of the baby is torn to pieces and then vacuumed out.

Abortion by suction is done between the 6th and the 12th weeks of pregnancy. This method is accomplished by introducing a tube through the cervix (the opening of the uterus), that is connected to a strong vacuum that destroys the body of the baby while it extracts it. Then, with the same tube, or with a curette (a curved knife made of steel) the abortionist cuts out the placenta from the wall of the uterus and extracts it. Nearly 95% of abortions use this method. Often the different parts of the body can be clearly identified. (Taken from www.vidahumana.com)

I am aware of the fact that these images may cause sensitive souls to recoil in horror, for that is how we react when a human being is torn apart and strewn over the ground in an accident, a robbery or war. They are horrible images.

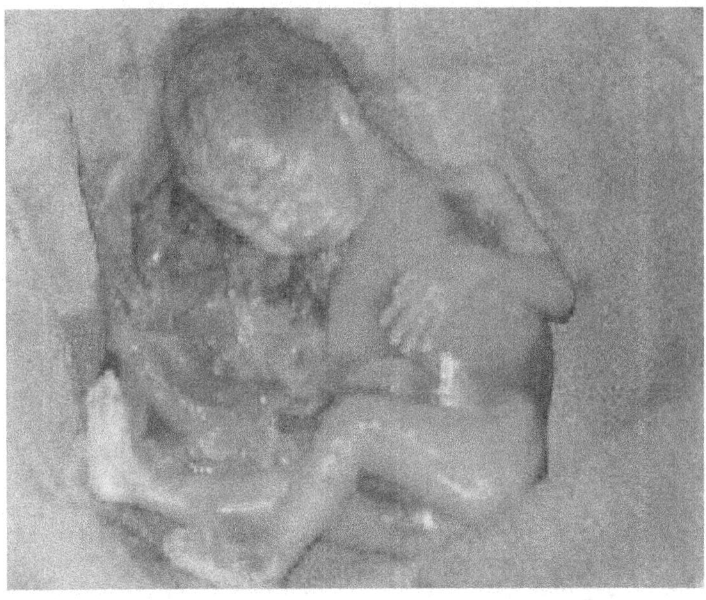

Another method of destroying the baby that is in its mother's womb is salt poisoning.

After the 16th week, a large needle is introduced in the mother abdomen until it penetrates the amniotic sack. Then a sat solution is injected, poisoning the baby when it breathes and swallows the solution. It is a slow process that takes over an hour to kill the baby. The mother will have labor pains about 24 hours later and this will pass the "product of the pregnancy".

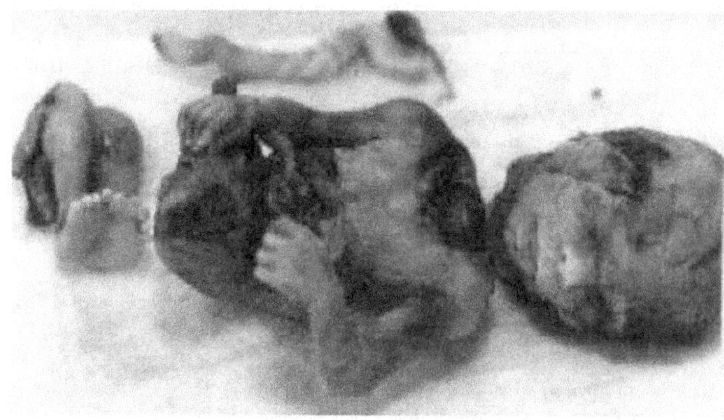

In this picture the baby is 19 weeks old. The introduction of the salt solution poisons the baby when it swallows it. Its skin is burnt by the caustic acid that is used to clean the remnants from the metal instruments and corrosive materials. The baby suffers for over an hour as it dies slowly.

This picture is from an abortion using the dilation and evacuation method on a 7 to 12-week-old baby A surgical knife shaped like a sickle cuts the baby's body in pieces and then it is extracted.

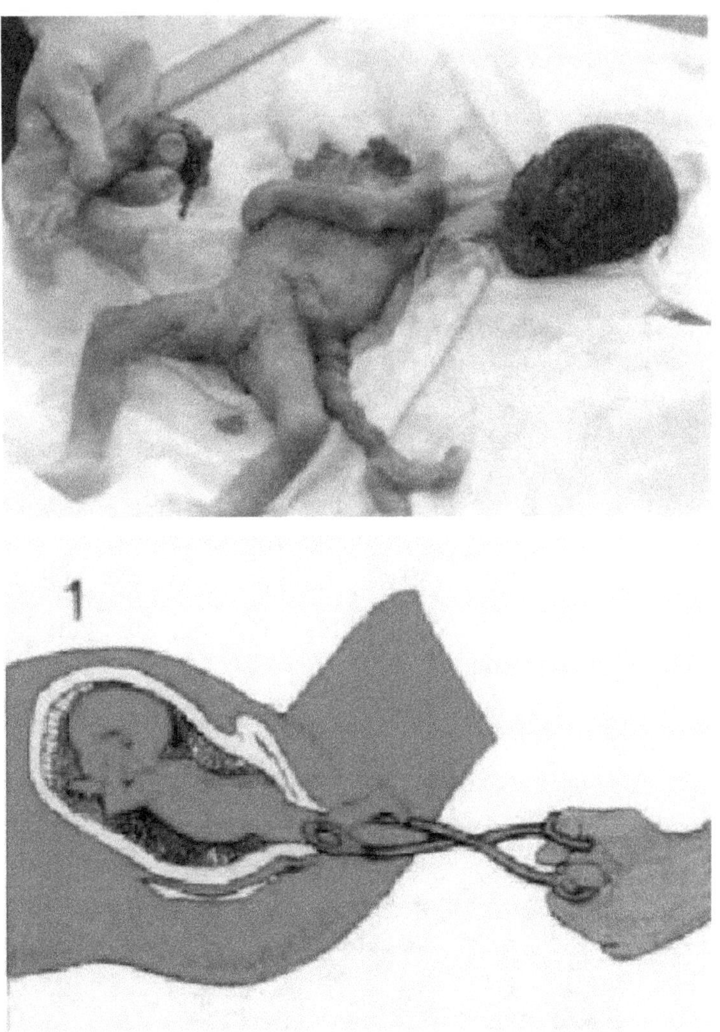

Partial birth abortion starts when the doctor takes hold of the baby within its mother's womb using forceps.

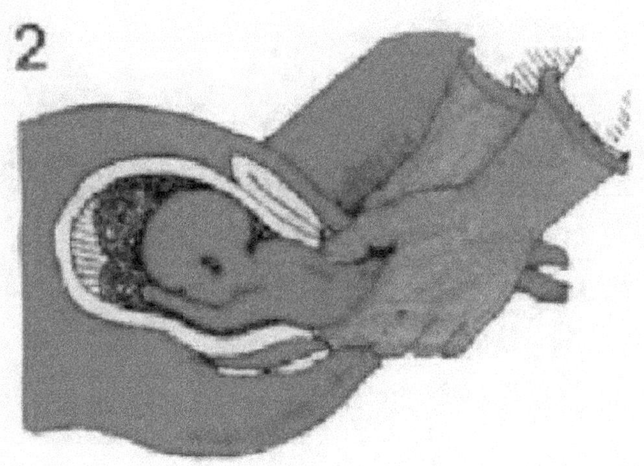

When the baby's feet are out of the uterus, the abortionist grabs a hold of it with his hands and takes it out, as if it were a natural birth, but making sure that the feet come out first.

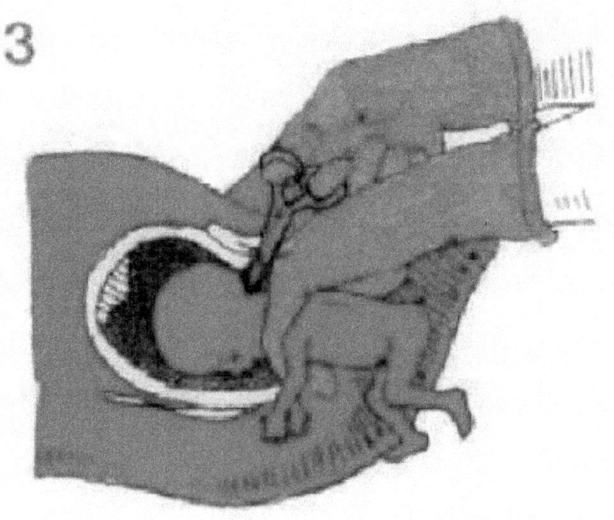

When the baby's body is out of the womb but the head still inside, the abortionist punctures its neck with a pair of scissors.

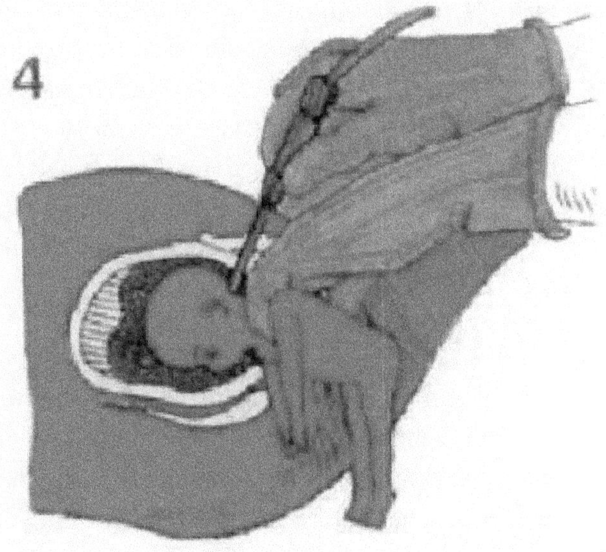

The crime concludes when the abortionist, using a catheter, suctions out the baby's brain matter. During the whole process, the baby's body is writhing about in a futile attempt to defend itself.

Abortion by «D and E»

This method is the most shocking of all. It is also known as **partial birth abortion**. It is usually done when the baby is about to be born.

After the uterus is dilated for three days, the abortionist, guiding himself by an ultrasound, introduces forceps into the uterus and grabs on to a leg, then the other one, after which follows the body, until he reaches the arms and shoulders of the baby.

Thus the body is partially extracted, as if it were a natural birth, except that the head is left inside the uterus. As the head is too big to come out in one piece, the abortionist punctures the base of the, yet live, baby's skull with a pair of scissors and opens them to enlarge the hole. Then he inserts a catheter connected to a vacuum and sucks out the brain. This procedure causes the baby to die and the head to collapse. Then the fetus is extracted and the placenta cut.

Abortion by Cesarean

This method is the same as the birth by cesarean section until the umbilical cord is cut. The difference is that instead of caring for the newborn, it is left to die. In abortion by cesarean, the idea is not to save the baby, but to kill it.

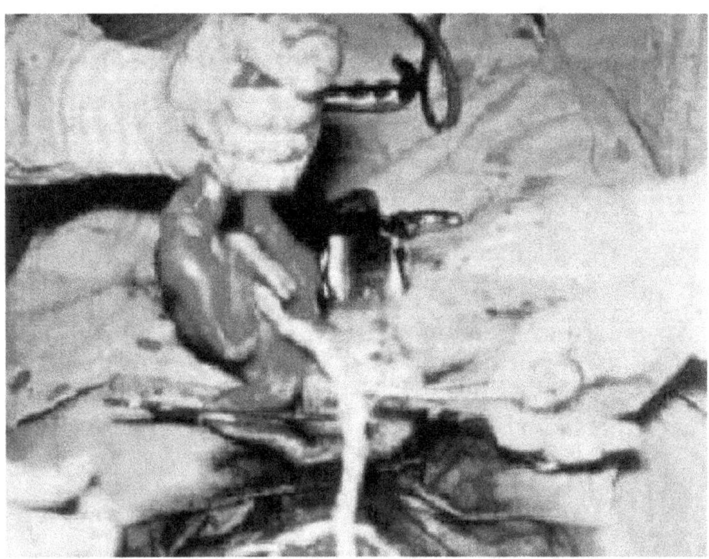

Abortion with Prostaglandin

The use of Prostaglandin produces an immediate birth at any stage of the pregnancy. It is used to induce an abortion in mid-pregnancy or in its later stages. The main problem with this method is that sometimes the baby is alive when it is born. It can also cause serious side effects on the mother. Prostaglandin has been used together with the RU-486 pill in order to enhance its "effectiveness".

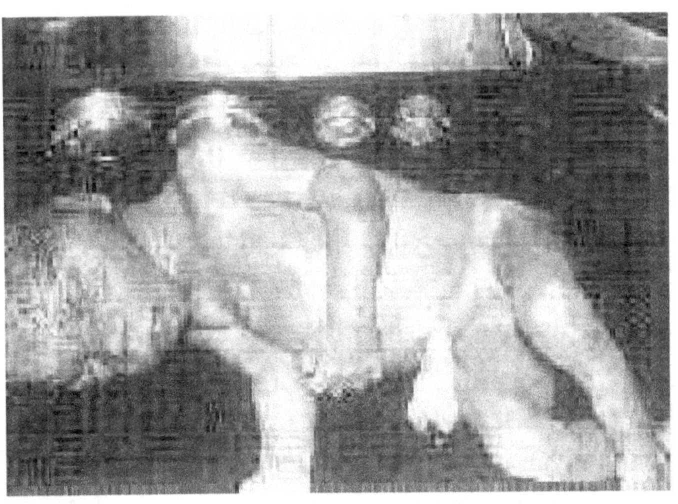

RU-486

This is an abortion drug used together with a prostaglandin. It is effective if used between the first and third week following the first time that the mother misses her menstrual period. It starves the tiny baby by depriving it of a vital element, the hormone progesterone. The abortion then comes after several days of painful contractions.

WHAT HAPPENS TO THE ABORTED FETUSES?

In many countries, aborted fetuses are in high demand. They are used for experiments or are sold to the cosmetic industry for the manufacture of beauty products with a collagen base. For some people, abortion is big business.

This is what is known as complicity. These company use the fetuses, knowing full well that most of them are the product of an induced abortion, but they don't care about the method used.

Imagine your baby boy or baby girl becoming a facial cream, bath soap, or some other body care item.

This is the same method and the same raw material used by the Nazis in the Second World War when they killed the Jews. They used the bodies to produce soaps, ointments, and other items.

The world today is demanding justice for that barbarism, but who speaks out in opposition to the legal and clandestine barbarism happening in the murder of babies so that their bodies might be used for the same purposes?

The law is tough in some countries such as the United States for murder and other capital offenses, often sending felons to the electric chair, the gas chamber, or condemning them to death by lethal injection, but who condemns abortion with such severity?

The problem is that what God has called evil, human beings think of as good; and what for God is abnormal, man considers normal. What for God is life, for man is death.

Recently, Al Rojo Vivo (Red Hot), a television show aired by one of the top Spanish-Language Television Networks, shoes that in the Middle East some of the wealthy host banquets in which they serve as a main dish the bodies of recently aborted babies.

Though it sounds crazy, it is a sad reality. Cannibalism has always existed, but in this case this sin has become a mockery of the whole human race, especially of those parents and doctors who allow it. How far will the depraved and defiant human mind go?

THE TORTURE OF A MEMORY

Such barbarism isn't just found on the streets of Brooklyn, or similar places in other countries, but is taking place in legal and illegal abortion clinics throughout the world.

This happens more than we know. There is an entirely too large a number of fetuses that are killed or that have their organs torn to shreds. For a woman getting an abortion, the memory of seeing her child in pieces on a tray would be sheer torture.

I am aware of the fact that the language here, as well as the images, is shocking. But it is the best way to reveal the truth about abortion, since many of those opting for an abortion are at best, uninformed. As has been pointed out, sometimes a couple seeking an abortion thinks that the fetus is nothing more than muscle and tissue, but are unaware of the suffering that the abortion produces, or the guilt that lingers long after the act is done.

Sometimes the trauma is terrifying. The memory of the child who could have been will never go away. The remorse is fierce and can even lead the individual to consider suicide de. I would advise you not to make such an extreme decision because the hope of forgiveness and restoration is always available.

A number of men and women, unable to bear the guilt have taken their own lives. That is never the best solution. God is quick to forgive and blot out the memory in spite of the mistake. God's mercy is never-ending. What matters is that the mistake not be repeated.

What is required is a decision like that of those who gave their testimonies in chapter 4: **"Never Again"**.

Anyone can ask a doctor, or a pediatrician, or a midwife about the life that is created at the moment of conception.

Maybe the concept can be better grasped by recognizing that when a woman becomes pregnant, she is giving life to another human being like herself. That is to say, she is a life that gives life.

On the one hand, it is exciting to have such a direct role in an event that is so sublime. God gives that privilege to human beings and animals. On the other hand, it can result in a great deception that can traumatize those involved, be it the man or the woman, due to the flesh and blood kinship and the responsibilities that it creates.

These are the main reasons why anyone with an unwanted pregnancy should be calm and not rush into a hasty decision. It is important to think it out, and seek spiritual and psychological counsel so that the pregnancy can be resolved appropriately.

There is always a solution, even if at first there may be some changes and hard decisions to be made. The important thing is not to destroy the life of a child. Certainly, as time passes, it will become evident that what seemed to be a curse has become just the opposite, a source of blessing.

As for the risks, those always exist. Yet we know that any father or mother would want to protect a child from a robbery, or a kidnapping, or an accident where the child is at risk for his or her life. Or would they let them be killed and die? Even if the child were the product of a rape, one crime doesn't justify another. Under any circumstances, ***abortion is definitely murder*** and those who practice it will not be immune to the torture of the memory of it.

CHAPTER 7

Abortion, the Bible and Christians

ABORTION AMONG THE PEOPLES OF THE BIBLE

Althrough the 6th commandment "Thou shalt not kill" does not specifically refer to the issue of abortion, it implies it. The Bible declares in Exodus 21: 22-23:

> *"If men fight, and hurt a woman with child, so that she gives birth prematurely, yet no harm follows, he shall surely be punished accordingly as the woman's husband imposes on him...But if any harm follows, then you shall give life for life".*

While the above passage does not allude the unborn, if it were to die, it is understood that the penalty the father of the child would impose would be the appropriate punishment for the loss of its life. This then implies a penalty for abortion provoked by others.

THE FACT THAT THE OLD TESTAMENT SELDOM MENTIONS ABORTION DOES NOT MEAN IT CONDONES IT

• Life is considered the greatest gift.

• Children are always a blessing.

• God knows man from the time he is in his mother's womb.

• Sterility was considered a curse in old testament times.

• The need to legislate about abortion was not necessary because its practice was uncommon.

The New Testament View on Abortion and Infanticide

A believer's hope does not only encompass a long life on earth and having many children, but reconciliation with God.

To not have children will never cease being a curse.

Our Lord Jesus addresses those who embrace sexual abstinence "for the kingdom of heaven's sake." (Matthew 19:12).

The apostle Paul acknowledges it is good to get married, but it is just as good to remain single as he did. (Please see 1 Corinthians 7: 7-9).

In the face of a pagan society that accepted and performed on a continuous basis termination of pregnancy and infanticide, early Christians openly favored life and took position of respect toward pregnant women and their babies.

According to Roman laws, a father had absolute authority over his children. Not only was he able to kill the fetus in its mother's womb, if he so desired, but he also had the right to kill the newborn if it was not pleasing to him.

As for the Greek, since everyone was a subordinate for the sake of society's well-being, they accepted abortion and infanticide as methods to regulate overpopulation.

Hippocrates, the father of medicine, rejects abortion in his Hippocratic Oath:

> *"...Similarly, I will not give to a woman an abortive remedy. In purity and holiness I will guard my life and my art."*

Clasical Version Text,

translation from the Greek, and Interpretation by Ludwig Edelstein

Baltimore: Johns Hopkins Press, 1943

The Hippocratic Oath is one of the oldest binding documents in history. Written in antiquity, its principles are held sacred by doctors to this day: treat the sick to the best of one's ability, preserve patient privacy, teach the secrets of medicine to the next generation, and so on. Today, most graduating medical school students swear to some form of the oath, usually a modernized version. Indeed, oath taking in recent decades has risen to near uniformity, with just 24 percent of U.S. medical schools administering the oath in 1928 to nearly 100 percent today.

On the other hand, Matthew, the evangelist, refers to the infanticide committed by Herod as a horrible act in relation to the prophecy of the Prophet Jeremiah:

"A voice was heard in Ramah,

Lamentation, weeping, and great mourning,

Rachel weeping for her children,

Refusing to be comforted,

Because they are no more."

(Matthew 2:18; Jeremiah 31:15)

Jesus teachings denote that:

• The Kingdom of God belongs to the children

• Mysteries hidden from the wise and prudent are revealed to the children

• Out of the mouth of babes and nursing infants He has perfected praise

Inasmuch, "as you did it to one of the least of these, you did it to me." (Matthew 25:40). If divine providence is so meticulous, how can abortion not be an offense to the Creator of life!

The emphasis Christ placed on the children unveils his zeal for them and the importance He gave to the little ones. Therefore, we can come to the conclusion that abortion was not a viable alternative for Him.

Let us examine the opinion of philosophers and prominent Christians about abortion:

Philo of Alexandria (13 b.C. to 54 a.C.) openly declared his opposition to the practice of abortion and infanticide by saying: "If a woman is having strong labor pains and is risking her life, it is permissible to destroy the child in her womb and extract each of its limbs because the life of the mother has priority; but if the child has been born, a life cannot be taken for the sake of another."

Flavio Josefo (37-100 a.C.) mentioned that: "The law provides that all children receive education and forbids a woman from getting an abortion; a woman who is found guilty of this crime is a child-killer because she destroys soul and diminishes the raze (Jonefo, Against Aplon, I:202).

Tertullian (155-220 a.C.) affirmed: "For us, because homicide is prohibited, it is not lawful to destroy the fetus inside the uterus. To prevent its birth is to accelerate a homicide, and there is no difference between taking a life that has been born or is about to be born. Because the latter is also a man. (Tertuliano, Eulogy, IX: 8I).

Juan Calvin (1509-1564) declared: "If a woman ejects the fetus from the uterus through the use of drugs, commits crime which is considered unpardonable." (Calvino, Open quae supersunt omnia, Brunsvigae, 1863-1900 XXII: 495)

Dietrich Bonhoeffer (1906-1945), said: "To kill the embryo in the mother's womb is to violate God's given right to the life that's in state of gestation. The debate as to whether it is already a life, or not, merely camouflages the simple fact that: God created a man whose birth was intentionally prevented. This is nothing more than murder." (Etica, 1968)

Karl Barth (1886-1968) affirmed: "Whoever destroys a life that is in state of gestation, kills a human being; It has the boldness, the monstrous desire of arbitrarily disposing of the life of a neighbor, of taking a life and destroying it as it belonged to him; forgetting that God is the only one who owns it because it was He who gave it" (Kirchliche Dogmatik 19321964 vol. 16).

The majority of Christians believe that:

• The human embryo has a spiritual nature far above its physical or bodily one because it was created in God's image;

• The human embryo is a human being from the moment of conception; therefore, we must respect its life because Christ also died for it;

• There is human life from the moment of conception, but the embryo develops its personal and distinctive features from its nature as a unique and indivisible being.

The Bible teaches that even life's most bitter experiences can be beneficial and later turn into a blessing.

And we know that all things work together for good to those who love God..." (Romans 8:28).

Early Christians' beliefs were in line with their faith and defense of life, by blatantly opposing to abortion. To be anti-abortion is to make a way for women who go through their pregnancy feeling lonely and destitute.

Anti-abortion practices can also yield benefits:

• Promote better sexual education among teens;

• Increase building of centers/clinics that offer psychological, spiritual, legal and financial aid to women in need;

• Facilitate adoption of children;

• Subsidize families of handicapped children.

What's important is not only to condemn abortion, but to spread the Gospel of Jesus Christ so that the sad reality of abortion will not have a place in our society.

Confirming the anti-biblical nature of abortion is the number hidden in the anti-abortion drug RU 486. If we subtract 2, from 8 we have 6. Then, add 2 to 4, and we will have six. The result: 666, is the number of the Antichrist (see graph below)

$$
\begin{array}{ccc}
4 & 8 & 6 \\
+2 & -2 & \\
\hline
6 & 6 & 6
\end{array}
$$

The above clearly reveals that abortion, or any method employed to prevent the birth of a child is contrary to Christ's principles and therefore, completely satanic.

WHAT DOES GOD THINK ABOUT ABORTION?

Believe me, those who are in favor of abortion, are uninformed, at best.

Abortion is a matter of great concern to God. He makes his voice heard throughout the world, claiming the lives of those He has created, through men and women who favor life.

Today, as a result of listening to this voice, in obedience and asking for His inspiration, I write about God's opinion of abortion.

Every person, of any nation, no matter what their culture or religion is, knows that abortion is about getting rid of something that can become a problem or a burden. It doesn't take into account that the life that has been conceived and is in the womb is in their likeness - Someone who is born from their inward parts. They were created the same way, through the intervention of two beings.

While traveling the world, I have noticed that human beings are different in their appearance: tall and short; white, yellow, black; with different languages, beliefs, costumes and traditions. However, their way of thinking, feelings, struggles and goals are the same, in America, Europe, Asia, Africa and in any part of the world.

This means that, in essence, human beings are the same in their principal characteristic: their heart.

At some point, Jesus said:

> *"Not what goes into the mouth defiles a man; but what comes out of the mouth, this defiles a man." (Matthew 15:11).*

> *"...For out of the abundance of the heart, the mouth speaks." (Matthew 12:34).*

Several times, in the Old Testament as well as in the New Testament, God speaks about the human heart referring to the attitudes resulting from its intentions.

Undoubtedly, it is within the heart where good or bad decisions are conceived. When He refers to the heart, He is not referring to the palpitating muscle which purpose is to pump blood to give life to the entire body, but rather to the hub within man where his feelings, desires, intentions and drives palpitate.

The heart, the one that is related to the mind and the intelligence, makes a human being similar to God. Therefore, if a heart is pure, the attitudes will be pure. If there is love in the heart, then love is what's going to emerge from that person. But, if there is selfishness, scorn, fears and prejudice, then all of those feelings will inevitably outcrop and lead to death, as opposed to life.

While God, since before the foundation of the world has been busy giving life to men, men, being influenced by a being called the devil, have taken it upon themselves to give death. Yes, allow me to assure you that abortion is simply diabolic. God always creates. Satan destroys and kills.

I firmly believe that only those whose conscience is hardened would commit such an act of violence and murder knowing that what they're doing is against God's principle to create.

CHAPTER 8

Conscience and Deliverance

CONSCIENCE AND MARTHA'S LITTLE DOG

Martha gave the pastor of the church where she had been going for years, a beautiful little dog.

After several months, the pastor noticed that Martha's little dog played, ran, leaped, ate and slept, but never barked. So, then one Sunday after the service, the pastor approached Martha and said to her:

"Dear, the dog that you gave me is beautiful, but I noticed it has never barked."

"Oh," said Martha, "I know what's wrong with it. This little dog, from the time it was little, used to bark nonstop, but one day I got tired of it and I stroke it on its head several times until it stopped barking."

This is what many people have done to their conscience. One day they stroke it and never heard it speak again.

Conscience is what God placed in human beings to direct their actions. However, many wishing to live as they please have silenced the voice of their conscience without realizing that it will speak out one day before the Creator.

CONSCIENCE AND THE BLACK BOX

Conscience is somewhat similar to that famous black box that airplanes carry. The Black Box is a computer that registers in an endless tape all the flight activities from the time the plane takes off to the time it lands and its engine is shut off.

Sometimes after a plane crash, the first thing that the airline's technicians do, after rescuing any survivors, is to look for the black box. When they find it, they take it to a lab to be activated. Once activated, the black box will reveal the truth about the causes of the crash. Witness and survivors have, most likely, given their statements. However, for the airline's management and investigators, what stands is what the black box shows.

Likewise, the consciences of many will face God when these are activated. Many will see themselves on a giant screen committing adultery, fornications, murders, rapes, abortions, etc. and in a desperate attempt will try to den they committed these sins. However, their consciences will condemn them because these don't lie, they tell the absolute truth.

Dear reader: I would like to emphasize that it is neither my intention nor my right to condemn you, but I must tell you the truth about abortion. I know that the cry, from their mothers' womb, of millions of infants who have been destroyed and disposed of, has touched God's heart. I have been merely called to stop such a wicked and satanic act. As Jesus said: the devil has come to steal, kill and destroy.

OTHER REASONS WHY SOME UNDERGO ABORTIONS

In the case of animals, we know that a female animal conceives through intervention of the male animal. As it relates to people, with the exception of Jesus Christ who was conceived of the Holy Spirit, God creates life in the womb of a woman through the intervention of a man. This is known as a natural and biological process that has been established since the beginning of creation by God. However, many people have lost sight of, or have never taken into account this principle.

Some consider that neither God, Jesus nor the Holy Spirit have something to do with this matter, because due to ignorance or for having paid attention to demonic doctrines, firmly believe that they have the free hand to take a life or to allow it to live. There is only one truth: We all have a right to give life but not to take it away, especially if it's an innocent, defenseless child.

Others, while ignoring the warnings about judgment and condemnation by God, consider abortion a normal and culturally-accepted procedure.

In this regard, this is a not a debate about existing doctrines and religions. Many of these religions deem that all ways lead to God and teach that God has made the decision not to intervene in certain aspects related to the development of humanity. To those who have such beliefs, I advise them that they're completely wrong.

GOD ALMIGHTY

Let's take a look at some of God's virtues... He is

Omnipresent

This means He has the ability to be in any place in the universe, in each instant of life, at the same time.

All-knowing

He has the ability to know about all possible and real things, including man's most intimate thoughts, in any place in the world.

All-powerful

He has enough power to change circumstances, to work miracles that no human being could do, and because He, through the power of His word, is the creator of the entire universe and its contents.

He who does not acknowledge the Almighty and all of His attributes does not fear God. This is the most serious problem distressing society today.

In 1990, while returning from the city of Salta, after an evangelistic crusade, the car I was traveling on broke down in the middle of the road. As we were trying to fix it, a woman approached us. I noticed she was a prostitute. Almost instantly, I handed her a pamphlet entitled "Are you Happy"?

That woman read a few lines, and then suddenly, her eyes were brimming with tears. She asked sobbing: "Do you think God can forgive me? Do you know about the terrible things I have done? Do you know who I am?"

"I don't know who you're or what you've done", I answered her. "I only know that the same God, who forgave my sins and delivered me, is the same God who can now do it with you."

We were all able to see about the great change and deliverance taking place in that woman. Her sadness and anguish turned into peace and happiness.

I have good news for you. It doesn't matter the horrendous sins you have done within your body, or how much doubt you have in your mind about your dignity and that of your child. The Word of God in Hebrews 9:14 mentions that the blood of Christ shed on the cross has power to cleanse your consciences from dead works.

If you are a woman and committed the sin of aborting a child, or if you're a man who got a woman pregnant or committed some other sin, there's still hope to get right with God. He will always give you another opportunity if after repenting, you humble yourself and accept His forgiveness.

On some occasion a woman was caught in adultery.

The gospel of John, in John 8:3-11 makes mention of it:

> *"Then the scribes and Pharisees brought to Him a woman caught in adultery. And when they had set her in the midst, They said to Him, "Teacher, this woman was caught in adultery, in the very act. Now Moses, in the law,*

Jewish law provided that any woman caught in such an act would die stoned. As men were persecuting her, she ran into Jesus and He forgave her and asked her to sin no more.

WHEN WE REPENT, THERE IS NO CONDEMNATION

As long as there is repentance, God will not condemn you nor will He allow shame to overpower you. On the contrary, the mere fact that you are willing to receive a child to take care of it, educate it and sustain it, will be a blessing. God will reward you.

For many women is a disgrace not to have children. This then confirms that the circumstances under which a child is conceived does not matter as a child always gives honor to its parents.

As to all matters concerning raising a child, do not be afraid of changes. Trust Jesus with all of your heart and allow the Holy Spirit to be your guide always.

Before murdering your baby, it is better to bring it into the world. If you're unable to take care of it, you can give it up for adoption by parents who would love it and take care of it.

Job, in his anguish, cried out:

"O why was I not hidden like a stillborn child, like infants who never saw light"? Job 3:16

Believe me, Job knew very well what he was talking about. Back in those days, hundreds of years before Christ, or even before creation dawned, the lives of defenseless children were destroyed in their mothers' wombs.

Truly, I don't think it is worthwhile to debate how many years this practice has been in existence. But, note that Job refers to it, even hundreds of years before Christ mentions it, which leads us to believe that abortion has been carried out since very ancient times.

Job was going through a though trial in his life, and felt that it would have been better for him to have been buried like a stillborn child, like a child who never saw the light of day. On some other occasion, Job cursed the day of his birth (please see Job 3: 1-3).

Beyond doubt, Job was desperate on account of the cruel circumstances he was undergoing and which he believed to be a curse. As a result, the best solution he finds in order to avoid his suffering is to have been buried and aborted.

Job did not realize he was a part of God's plan, that he was chosen. Someone, with whom, from the time he was in his mother's womb and even before that, God had a purpose.

God, given his eternal nature and his ability to know about the present and the future, determined that Job would not be aborted. If we read the book of Job, we will notice that far beyond the curse Job complained of, there was a great blessing reserved for his life. (See Ephesians 1: 3-6).

Dear friend, abortion is a decision that will bring about curses.

It is a curse because not only does it cause the ill effect of death, but consequences for the rest of your life. It will bring on a horrible burden of guilt for having killed someone defenseless and for no reason. Remember, after death came, God hand to curse the earth. (Please see Genesis 3:17 b).

CREATION OF GOD

Note that Job also says: ".. a stillborn child, like those children who never saw light (Job 3:16). Undoubtedly, with this affirmation he acknowledges that the stillborn is a child, a creation of God. In other words, it is a being that has been created with a spirit, soul and body.

It has a spirit, because without it, it wouldn't have life. From the very moment that spirit is gestating in its mother's womb, it has life. The spirit is the first to be born. Then the body begins to take shape while the soul, at the same time, gives it feelings.

Note the following from the Holy Scriptures, in Genesis 2:7:

> *"And the Lord God formed man of the*
> *dust of the ground, and breathed into*
> *his nostrils the breath of life, and man*
> *became a living being"*

Although the first man and woman were created by God's hands, it is key to understand that all of us who followed are also His creation. While conception comes about through the intervention of a man and a woman, the breath of life, or spirit, comes from God.

Job 32:8 states:

> *But there is a spirit in man, and the breath of the Almighty gives him understanding.*

While Psalm 139:13-16 (NIV version) declares:

> *"For you formed my inward parts; You covered me in my mother's womb. I will praise You, for I am fearfully and wonderfully made: Marvelous are Your works, And that my soul knows very well. My frame was not hidden from You, When I was made in secret, And skillfully wrought in the lowest parts of the earth. Your eyes saw my substance, being yet unformed. And in Your book they all were written, The days fashioned for me, When as yet there were none of them".*

In the book of the Prophet Jeremiah we can see a more profound revelation denoting that every created being had life even before conception took place. God says in Jeremiah 1:5:

> *"Before I formed you in the womb I knew you; before you were worn I sanctified you..."*

The above passage reveals that it is God who sends every human being to this world. This means that children belong to God and that He sends them as a blessing for the world. Therefore, the guilt and accountability before God are much greater, since through abortion, we destroy the life of someone whom God sends to be protected, educated and formed. We can clearly come to the conclusion that abortion rejects and scorns a gift given by God.

THAT CREATED BEING IS WORTHY OF ADMIRATION

When a baby is born, a multitude of angels surround it for it's a wonderful work of God. Its bones, tissues, muscles, hands, legs, eyes, mouth and ears and each and every one of its organs are perfect.

All the days in its life have already been planned by God. Yet, this that doesn't mean that God has made us like robots, rather that He gave us the right to choose. God knows about every one of His children footsteps. And everything that occurs in our life is because He allows it.

Certainly, every human being is a creation of God.

It is an absolute lie that life is formed from the evolution of atom, or from a monkey. Believe me, monkeys beget monkeys, giraffes beget giraffes, and so on. Such erroneous way of thinking has deceived millions of people as it misleads them from the truth. As a consequence, they've made God a liar and turned their backs on their Creator.

The passage from the book of Psalms mentioned earlier affirms that the being inside a woman's womb is formed by God's hands. This creation is considered the most wonderful of all. This is to say that every human being that is conceived is precious and valued. Nothing has more value for God than His created beings.

We can infer that as the Omnipresent God, His eyes are, since the time of Creation, upon every man and woman, and upon their walk.

Lastly, it acknowledges that all the life of a human being, from conception to death, it is written in His book. Consequently, man's life has been established by God.

In Psalm 127:3-5, we read:

> *"Behold, children are a heritage from the Lord, The fruit of the womb is a reward. Like arrows in the hand of a warrior, So are the children of one's youth. Happy is the man who has his quiver full of them; They shall not be ashamed. But shall speak with their enemies in the gate".*

A son or a daughter is a blessing. We should not be afraid to bring him or her into the world. God has promised to protect them. He will never allow a mother or a father, whether single or married, to be ashamed of their children. On the contrary, they will receive honor from God.

As to the spirit, the breath of God is what gives it understanding. If there is understanding, there are feelings!

When a man or a woman makes the decision to seek an abortion, they cancel and dispose of that created being who has received a spirit that belongs and comes from God.

As to the feelings of that created being, they're exactly the same to those of any human being of this world.

As to the body, as you attempt to obliterate or destroy it, though it's not fully formed yet, it feels the same pain that any human being feels when a knife is thrust, a bullet penetrates, or when other parts of the body are cut off.

CURSES BROUGHT ON AS A RESULT OF INTENTIONAL ABORTION

The first curse that is brought on is the terrible burden of remorse that people bear due to the cry of that being who was destroyed.

To just think that baby could have been humanitarian to society, or someone whom God would ha used to bring millions out of misery and wickedness, can cause a great sense of remorse.

I have known of cases where they've had to endure, due to having performed an abortion, sufferings because of sickness, financial losses, destruction of families, disputes, persecutions.

Other consequences that can destroy the life of those who undergo abortions are post-abortion infections, some of them so serious that can even lead up to sterility and death. There is even the possibility of being infected with AIDS due to the use of non-sterilized instruments.

The absence of peace is also a curse generated by abortion. The devil is every active in these cases. There are people who are oppressed by demons because the sin of abortion, like any other sin, opens doors to unclean spirits, thereby giving them the right to bring on torment.

On some occasion, for hours, we were trying to deliver a woman who was being oppressed by evil spirits, without much success. I perceived there was something hidden related to her past. When I asked her if she had at some point in her life undergone an abortion, she responded affirmatively. After confessing and repenting before God, she was freed in just a few minutes from the demons that were tormenting her. Her life was completely changed. You may have to consider if the many sufferings that are activated in your life are due to the curses resulting from abortion.

INTENTIONAL ABORTION AND PHYSICAL CONSEQUENCES

Any medical professional knows about the high risks that a mother takes when undergoing an intentional abortion.

The principal cause of deaths in Argentina is intentional abortion.

Though we have already touched on the high risks associated with abortion, we'll expand on this reality. Those risks include infections that can affect your entire body, organ decay, cancer and even death.

As we have seen in the photographs in an earlier chapter, by brutally inserting sharp objects inside the body, germs and infections are attracted. The wounds in the body of a mother can cause pain and sicknesses. These sicknesses perhaps are not life-threatening, but become chronic in the spiritual, physical and emotional areas.

All of these consequences will not only affect the guilty ones but those who are around them. For example, when someone becomes handicapped, those who live with, or are around that person are affected by such sickness and the sickness will eventually turn into a burden.

The world undergoes suffering because it has been bearing the heavy burdens of curses. Curses that have been caused by their uncontrolled life style and freedom. They have a name: **It's sin.**

*For all of these reasons, and many more, and especially because it is a sin of murder, please **say no to abortion** as it is a totally satanic act.*

If you have been thinking about getting an abortion or if you've already undergone one, before God this is a sin like many others. But, I have good news. No matter what your sins may have been, like that woman we mentioned earlier and who couldn't believe that God would forgive her, God's own son, Jesus Christ, gave his life on the cross to deliver us from all condemnation. Isaiah 53:5 (NIV) says:

> *"But He was wounded for our transgressions; He was bruised for*

our iniquities; The chastisement for our peace was upon Him, and by His stripes we're healed".

Jesus Christ was beaten, tortured, and bruised for our rebellions. But He gave himself up for love to His creation. Though lost, walking in our own ways, we're a part of His creation.

Rebellion and sin is what separates us from God. He is angry at sinners and rebels. However, Isaiah 55:6-7 (NIV) declares:

"Seek the Lord while He may be found, Call upon Him while He is near. Let the wicked forsake his way, And the unrighteous man his thoughts; Let him return to the Lord, and He will have mercy on him; And to our God. For He will abundantly pardon".

Abortion and rebellion are acts of perversion. If a person persists in these sins, they will run the risk that God will separate from them and will never be found.

For the foregoing reasons, dear friend, don't lose this opportunity. It doesn't matter what is your degree of wickedness, what counts is that there is still time to get right with God. Today is the day of salvation. Tomorrow may be too late!

The Bible says in Romans 6:23:

"For the wages of sin is death, But the gift of God is Eternal life in Christ Jesus our Lord"

Does it make sense to bear all of your life the burden of sin and a horrible expectation of judgment? What sense does it make to lose your life when God gives us the opportunity to reconcile with Him and thus receive eternal life?

The Day of Judgment will come. On this day, we will be put to shame and sent to hell, if we don't repent beforehand. The baby that you rejected and destroyed physically will most likely be present then. Know that man can kill the body but not the soul. That soul which will rise up in glory will be the one to condemn you.

Now is the time to repent and receive forgiveness. All you have to do is say a prayer, which just means to have a conversation with God.

Pray as follows:

Lord I acknowledge that I am a sinner y repent of all of my sins. I ask you to cleanse them through the blood of your son Jesus Christ. Sanctify me and restore me Before you. I ask that you help me to resist all temptations that come my way and to solve my problems. Deliver me and heal me of all of my weaknesses I ask this in the mighty name of Jesus Christ. Amen.

I invite you to visit a Christian church near your home. Pray, asking the Holy Spirit to guide you to the congregation where they will fulfill your needs. May God bless you abundantly.

Miguel Ángel Kircos

APPENDIX

"I PERFORMED FIRE THOUSAND ABORTIONS"

By Dr. Bernard N Nathanson

We were a group whose sole purpose was to see a law passed in the U.S. that would allow abortions. We put pressure on the members of Congress and the legislative bodies at the State level to repeal the laws that banned abortion. I was one of the founders of the largest organization that "sold" abortion to the American people.

When we organized the movement in 1968, it was estimated that less than 1% of the population of the U.S. participated in abortion on demand. Our annual budget then was $7,500, but by 1982 it was approaching a million dollars.

Let me explain how we tried to convince the American people to accept abortion. The tactics that we used are the same ones that have been used and are being used in other countries. Our strategy was based upon two big lies: the faking of statistics and surveys that we claimed to have done, and the choice of a scapegoat to take the blame for banning abortion in the U.S. That victim was the Catholic Church, or rather, its hierarchy of bishops and cardinals.

THE FORGING OF STATISTICS

This was an important tactic. In 1968, we said that a million illegal abortions were performed in the U.S., when we knew that the real figure was closer to a hundred thousand. But that figure was too small to be of much use, so to enhance the shock value we simply multiplied it by ten. We also repeated constantly that the death to the mothers in illegal abortions was nearly ten thousand, when we knew that it was under 200. But that figure was also too small to be of much use. If the lie is repeated enough, it comes to be accepted as the truth. We set out to gain the acceptance of the mass media by convincing university students, especially the feminists. They would listen to everything we said, including the lies, and then spread our propaganda to the mass media.

The mass media is of vital importance. If the media in Spain is not willing to tell the truth, then you are faced with the same situation that we created in the U.S.

We also made up our own surveys. We would say, for example, that we had conducted a survey in which 25% of the population approved abortion, then three months later we would say that the figure had risen to 50%, and so on. The American people believed it, and since they didn't want to appear old fashioned, they would join the "majority" of "forward thinkers" so as not to appear "backward."

Later, we did genuine surveys and were able to see that little by little, the results were approaching what we had invented. It is good then to be cautious about abortion surveys; because they may be conjured up.

90

They do however have the power to convince judges and legislators, because, like the rest of the public, they read the newspapers or listen to the radio or television, and take that into account.

THE CATHOLIC CHURCH SELECTED AS A SCAPEGOAT

One of the more efficient strategies that we used in those days was what we called the "Catholic label".

In 1966, the war in Vietnam was unpopular, but the Catholic Church in the United States supported it. It was then that we chose the Catholic Church to be our scapegoat and tried to relate it to other "reactionary", movements, including the antiabortionist movement. For that, we got the young people and the protestant churches that always been suspicious of the Catholic Church to turn against them. We managed to convince the people that the Catholic Church was responsible for preventing the approval of a pro abortion law.

Since it was important that we not create antagonism between Americans of different faiths, we targeted Catholic hierarchy - the bishops and cardinals - as the "bad guys". The Catholics who rejected abortion were accused of being "brainwashed" by the hierarchy, and those who accepted it were considered "modern", "progressive", "liberal" and more "enlightened". I can assure you that the problem of abortion is not a denominational issue. The Catholic Church is not the only religious institution that is against abortion. I don't belong to any denomination, and yet I am speaking out against abortion. But the strategy was so effective that it is now being used in other countries.

Another tactic that we used against the Catholic Church was to accuse its priests, whenever they took part in public debates against abortion, of "getting into politics", and that their stand was "unconstitutional". The public believed it readily, even though the fallacy of the argument is plain.

SINCE 1971 I MANAGED THE LARGEST ABORTION CLINIC IN THE WORLD

It was the Center for Sexual Health (CRANCH), located east of New York City. I directed 10 operating rooms and 35 doctors. When I took charge of the clinic everything was dirty and horribly unsanitary. The doctors were not washing their hands between abortions. Some of the abortions were even carried out by nurses or mere orderlies. I managed to change all of that and transform the clinic into a "model" in its class.

We performed 120 abortions every day, including Sundays. The only day we didn't work was Christmas. As Department Head, I must confess that 60,000 abortions were performed at my direction, and I personally performed some 5,000.

I remember that at one of the office parties, some of the wives of the doctors told me that their husbands had nightmares and would shout out loud as they visualized the blood and mangled bodies of the fetuses. Others drank too much or used drugs. Others had to undergo psychiatric treatment. A number of the nurses become alcoholics and others left the clinic in tears. For me, it was a life changing experience.

In September 1972, I submitted my resignation because I felt that my goal of getting the clinic in working order had been accomplished. Frankly, I didn't leave the clinic at that time because had anything against abortion; I left it because I had other agendas to fulfill. I was appointed Director of Obstetrics at New York's Saint Luke's Hospital and began to set up a fetology lab. By examining the fetus in its mother's womb, I was able to recognize that it was a human being with all its features and that they should be granted all the privileges and protections that are given to every citizen.

THE CONCLUSION I REACHED FROM THE STUDY OF THE LIVE FETUS

Inside the Uterus

You may think that as a doctor and a gynecologist I should know without examining it that the fetus is a human being. Essentially, I did know it, but I hadn't verified it scientifically myself. The new diagnostic tools gave us the ability to better recognize its human form and not consider it just a piece of tissue. With today's modern medical techniques, several fetal diseases can be treated in the uterus, and there are even 50 different types of surgical interventions that can be done. These are the scientific arguments that have changed my way of thinking. Imagine: if the fetus is a patient who can be treated, then it is a person, and if it is a person, then it has a right to life and our protection of it.

THE CASES OF RAPE, ABNORMALITY AND HEALTH OF THE MOTHER

Rape is a very painful situation. Fortunately, few rapes actually end up in pregnancy. But even so, rape, which is an act of unspeakable violence, must not be followed with another act just as unspeakable: the destruction of a living being. To try to cover up an act of horrible violence with another equally as horrific just does not seem logical. It is simply absurd, and what it actually does is to augment the trauma of the woman by destroying an innocent life. That life has value in itself even if it came about through atrocious circumstances, circumstances that could never justify its destruction. Many of those of us living now were conceived under circumstances that were less than ideal, maybe without love and human warmth, but that does not change us in the slightest nor does it brand us as disgraceful. Resorting to abortion, then, in cases of rape is illogical and inhuman.

With the advances in medicine today, there are practically no cases in which the life of the mother is jeopardized by allowing a pregnancy to continue. The argument for abortion then on the basis of the health of the mother is deceiving because it simply is not true.

Finally, let me consider the issue of abortion when the fetus will be born with defects. This is a very delicate subject because it means that we are wishing for a society made up of physically perfect people, and I can say unequivocally that there is no one in this room who is physically perfect. It is extremely dangerous to buy into this principle, because it would result in another holocaust.

Let me tell you a story. When I was with my wife in New Zealand, we had lunch one day with Sir William Liley, one of the foremost fetologists in the world. He told us that he had four children who were now grown, and now that he and his wife were alone, (they adopted a mongoloid child. He told me that this adopted child had given them more satisfaction than any of his other four children).

I can assure you that if this type of law is passed it will be abused and used to justify abortion in all cases. That is what has happened in Canada. The doctors simply sign off on the abortion requests and the whole world laughs at them and the ridiculous law. I think that when abortion is allowed, what is allowed is an act of mortal violence, an act of deliberate destruction and so, a crime. I can assure you that if we follow the bloody path of abortion, the three Horsemen of the Apocalypse which are delinquency, drugs and euthanasia, will soon be after us, as is already happening in the United States.

I would like to end with these words: As a scientist, I do not merely believe; I know that life starts at the moment of conception and should be preserved. If we neglect our dedication to such an important cause and fail to be victorious, history will never forgive us.

Editor's Note: The above has been excerpted from lecture that Dr. Bernard N. Nathanson gave at the Medical College in Madrid on November 5, 1982. It was published in "Fuerza Nueva" ["New Force"] magazine.

Dr. Nathanson was one of the foremost promoters of abortion in his country (U.S.A.) and a founding member of the National Association for the Repeal of Abortion Laws, or NARAL. His amazing conversion from pro-abortionist to pro-life and from atheist to believer is told in his recently published autobiography titled "The Hand of God". This fascinating book not only narrates God's wonderful work in the life of this man, but also takes a look, in the author's own words, at the insidious tactics of the pro-abortion movement in a more detailed and complete form. Every pro-life advocate should have the valuable information.

SOURCE: "I practiced five thousand abortions", a lecture given by Dr. Bernard Nathanson at the Medical College in Madrid on November 5,1982 and published in "Fuerza Nueva" ["New Force"] magazine. Dr. Nathanson was one of the foremost promoters of abortion in the United States and founding member of the National Association for the Repeal of Abortion Laws or NARAL. Currently, Dr. Nathanson is a pro-life lecturer converted to Christ

TESTIMONIES OF FORMER EMPLOYEES OF ABORTION CLINICS

• **Judith Fetrow:** PPFA volunteers or escorts (for women coming into the abortion clinics) as well as the employees have been told not to talk to pro-life Christians. They have been told this because too many employees and volunteers have heard the truth and have changed their ways.

• **Marian Johnston-Loehner**: Someone gave me a book written by Dr. Jean Garton titled "Who Broke the Baby?" This book took all of the euphemisms that I had been using for years as a pro-choice advocate and destroyed them one at a time. I read a little bit of it each night and would cry myself to sleep. The night that I finished reading it, the dam broke, the tears came and I repented. I grieved over everything that I had done, and was truly sorry to have taken the life of innocent children. Until then, even after the birth of my son and then the birth of my daughter, I was not willing to admit that a fetus is a human being from the time of conception. I had given in to the lies.

• **Dina Madsen**: I was assisting the doctor and gathering the dismembered parts of babies. The jokes and the sarcastic remarks which I had heard all the time I was there in the abortion clinic died down. I was changing to the point that I hated to be there, I hated going to work, to have to be in the same room with the abortionist and those women. I hated it, I wanted to run and scream.

• **Joy Davis**: When I was in the abortion industry, I started to have nightmares and to experience feelings of guilt because what I was doing was wrong. It was then that I went to talk to a friend at a nearby abortion clinic. I told him about the way I was feeling, the nightmares and the guilt. He told me that he understood it well, because he had also been having nightmares and feeling a tremendous sense of guilt.

Fourteen years ago they offered me a job at an abortion clinic in Birmingham, Alabama. I considered the offer, and assuming that it was a good thing and that I would be helping women by fighting for a just cause, I took the position. Shortly thereafter, I realized that it was not about helping women, but was a business, a money making scheme.

The conditions of the clinic where I worked were extremely poor. We did not own any life-saving equipment. The staff wasn't well trained. Most of them didn't even have any medical experience. The doctors came and went and so they were never the same ones.

I met a doctor in the clinic, Tommy Tucker, who told me one day that he wanted to open his own clinic and do things right. He wanted to have employees who were well trained and qualified. He wanted to use general anesthesia and bring in anesthesiologists, so the women would not suffer, because in the clinic where we worked the women suffered plenty.

I thought that his offer was a wonderful idea and agreed to work there. I became regional director of six abortion clinics in Mississippi and Alabama. We had the best equipment. The staff was well trained and efficient. We lied to the women, but that was necessary in order to earn money. And we saw only a few women each day, because we didn't want to rush them through like cattle. We wanted to take time with them and give them the kind of medical attention they needed.

After a few months, the doctor's greed surfaced. He thought that he wasn't making enough money, so he fired the anesthesiologists, because they were costing too much. With just a few months of having watched how the patients were anesthetized, we started to do it ourselves without even knowing what we were doing. We had just seen it done.

Then the nurses who worked in the recovery room were fired; then the lab technician, and so on.

I started to interview people with absolutely no medical knowledge, and hired them as anesthesiologists, lab technicians, nurses and even as doctors. We would bring in people from the street, without medical backgrounds, and would give them on the job training.

We saw approximately ten women a day in each clinic, but that wasn't enough. We started to see as many as we could. But there wasn't a plane fast enough to take the doctor to all of those clinics. So he trained me to be a doctor. I had never been in medical school, not even for a single day. I had only been trained as an ultrasound technician. My background was in business, and I didn't know anything about medicine, other than what I had seen done by other doctors over the years.

Then I started to perform abortions, surgeries, Norplants, cryosurgery, Pap smears, and pelvic exams. I was doing the same things that the doctor had done and was proud of myself because I thought I did it better. All of the employees were saying, "You need to see Dr. Davis today," because they thought that I was better doctor than he was. I never had any trouble with the patients. I never had to send a woman to the hospital, and he had sent women to the hospital nearly every month in critical condition for hysterectomies or residual tissue. Everything that could go wrong with his patients did.

I thought everything was going fine for me because I wasn't running into any of those problems. I took my time with my patients and treated them with much love. But I was risking their lives with my negligence. Of the thousands upon thousands of patients that we saw, I couldn't remember one name or face, because they had just become a number to me. I referred to them by the amount they had paid. "Oh, this is a case of four hundred dollars; this is a case of five thousand dollars." I didn't see them as people, just as numbers.

One day a young lady came to have an abortion late in the second trimester. We performed abortions to end pregnancies almost up to the time of birth. Dr. Tucker performed the abortion and then left the room almost immediately upon finishing. The girl was under general anesthesia administered by an unqualified individual.

I took her to the recovery room. I stayed with her there and did everything I could to stabilize her, but she started to bleed profusely and I couldn't stop it. So I hurried to find the doctor and ask him for help. When I found him I said, "She's bleeding and I don't know what to do." He answered, "Take her to the exam room, find out why she is bleeding and stop the hemorrhage. It's just that simple. I'm busy."

I did everything that I knew to do, but the bleeding continued. I called an ambulance to take her to the hospital. When the doctor found out, he got mad and canceled the ambulance. He told me, "I'm the doctor here and I'll make the decisions. I can't send a patient to the hospital in this shape, they'd hang me. Now try to stabilize her."

Blood was all over the place. It gushed out as if from a water faucet and I couldn't stop it. I asked the doctor to please take over, saying, "If you don't help me, this woman will die." He said, "OK, call an ambulance. I have a plane to catch." And with that, he left. Then I called the ambulance, which got there in twenty minutes. During that span of time I realized that I wasn't a doctor. Trying to save a life without knowing how to do it frightened me tremendously, and I wished I had never gone along with the farce.

What came to my mind was the idea that it was me who had considered this doctor as some kind of hero. He had managed to help me earn about a hundred thousand dollars a year. But at that moment I realized what he really was: a coward. He ran out on a patient when she needed him the most. She was taken to the hospital and I was glad because now she would be with doctors who could care for her properly and I was relieved of that responsibility, that is until the hospital called me to inform me of her death.

Then I started having nightmares. Every time I closed my eyes I could see her face. I felt so guilty about it. I was upset that the man that I had admired so much would have been so negligent, and that almost destroyed me.

Then the medical board asked for a report of the incident. The doctor went even further and changed them to avoid responsibility. He gave me originals of the chart and asked me to go to the basement and burn them. He said that we couldn't take them to Court because they would hang us. We had to cover up what really happened. He told me to burn the charts immediately, but I couldn't do it. I took the charts and put them in my file cabinet, because I knew that I shouldn't lie to get him off. I would no longer hide what he did.

So I went to the medical board and the district attorney's office. I gave them all the information about our negligence. I confessed to having practiced medicine without a license and provided the evidence of it. They asked me to continue as his employee, because they wanted to continue gathering information about him. They said that this case was clearly negligent homicide, but time passed and nothing was done about it.

One day Dr. Tucker came back to Alabama from Mississippi, where we met. He asked me to return to Mississippi because some problems had arisen in the clinic there and the employees needed to be calmed down. A girl had come in for an abortion. The doctor thought that she 18-weeks pregnant; but it turned out that she was closer the end of her pregnancy. When the light was inserted, she gave birth to a live and healthy baby. So I asked him, "What did you do then?" He responded, "What could I do? I killed the baby." Since all the employees were in an uproar, I needed to go and take care of it.

I caught a plane and went to Mississippi, but first I called the district attorney and told him what had happened. Before I could get to the clinic, he was already interviewing the employees. The case went to the grand jury, but they couldn't prove his guilt in the death of the baby, because the baby had disappeared. Even though the employees testified to what had happened, there was no proof.

I returned to the medical board in Alabama and asked them, "Why aren't you doing anything? Why haven't you done something about the death of this girl?" They indicated that abortion was such a hot political issue that they were afraid to touch it. The mass media got hold of that information and forced the medical board to take action against the doctor. He no longer had businesses in Mississippi and Alabama. They had suspended his license. The Department of Health closed down all of his clinics, and so he couldn't harm anyone else.

The driving force behind abortion is greed. Not only do they not care about the life of the baby, but neither do they care about the lives of the women getting abortions.

• **Joan Appleton**: There is no medical personnel in the independent clinics other than the doctor who performs the abortion. The doctors that we employed were either rookies who were just getting started in private practice and did abortions to earn enough money to make ends meet, or doctors who didn't earn much and so were working in the abortion clinic to pay for their malpractice insurance, which was exorbitantly high for gynecologists and obstetricians.

I usually advised the women that they should take birth control pills to avoid having to return for another abortion. I would give them their first package free, because the drug companies would give complimentary samples to the doctors.

We would give them a five-month supply along with directions for their use.

But outfits such as the PPFA and the abortion industry weren't stupid. They knew that the smaller the dose of estrogen in the pills, the greater the probability that they would fail, thus forcing women to come in for another abortion. So they would use pills with a 30% failure rate. We didn't forget to tell them that if they got the flu or a cold, they would need antibiotics. Then, the chemical interaction between the birth control pill and the antibiotic would render the birth control pill useless thereby increasing its failure rate by another 20%. At this point, they would need our services.

We would then go to the schools to teach the girls on how to have risk-free sex. We would lead them to believe that we were concerned for them. Those who are in the abortion industry now go to the schools and say, "Boys and Girls, we know that you will have sex; we understand that and it's OK." What we would not tell them is that when they did, two, three or four of them would die. But, by using our condoms and our birth control methods to have safe sex, only three to five of them would die - the rest would live. Of course, 30% of those would contract some kind of venereal disease, but then, friends, we were there to take care of that.

One of the things that always bothered me, even when I was head nurse at the clinic, is the great emotional trauma that those getting an abortion undergo... But if it is something natural and right, why is it so traumatic? I asked myself that all the time. And if I counseled these women so well and they were so sure of their decision, why would they come back to me months or years later in a state of psychological ruin?

Those of us who belonged to the 'pro-choice' movement and the abortion industry denied the existence of the post-abortion syndrome. Yet, it is real and in the face of the growing number of women who kept coming back, we couldn't deny its existence.

Also, I witnessed an abortion in which we used an ultrasound. It was late in the first trimester, or maybe the second trimester. I don't remember what the specific problem was, but we wanted to do the abortion with an ultrasound to be sure that we got the entire baby, or, in the lingo we used, the complete pregnancy. I ran the ultrasound machine and the doctor did the procedure as I was watching the screen and telling him what to do. The baby could be seen recoiling and opening its mouth. I had seen the Silent Scream, a video that shows an abortion, several times but was always unaffected by it. As far as I was concerned, it was just another piece of pro-life propaganda, but I couldn't deny what I was seeing on the screen. After the procedure was over with, although I was trembling, I managed to get through the rest of the day.

The office manager told me about the existence of a crematorium in that room. It was a big one like the funeral homes use. I just couldn't take it. There was a horrible gas smell when the oven was on. And the worst was that we could smell the babies burning, as my office was right around the corner

Every time that a woman came to have an abortion, or a dilatation and extraction (an abortion method), we would write it down on her chart. Some of them were filled on both sides, because the woman had had multiple abortions. And sometimes a doctor would see them and joke around by saying, "If they hurry, they can come again before Christmas." Does a person like that really care about the women? I don't think so.

• **Dina Madsen**: No medical knowledge was required for the position - just a willingness to perform abortions.

I saw the babies as disposable items. I didn't consider them important. I didn't value my own life, so how could I value the lives of others? And if these women were so stupid as to end up pregnant, then it was their own fault. That's what I thought, and so did the majority of the staff.

Some of the managers with whom I worked, had had eight or nine abortions, and [yet] they despised the women who would come in repeatedly for the same reason.

Of all the women with whom I worked, I would say that about half of them had had abortions, and some of them repeated times, but they would not allow any of the doctors at the clinic to touch them for any reason. And yet every day they would tell the women that came in how wonderful the doctors were, that they would do them no harm, that they were the best doctors in their field, that they were really nice, etc. Sometimes the women would ask, "Have you ever had an abortion?" And they would respond, "Yes, but he didn't do it."

I have to admit, though, that I didn't have much sympathy (for the women who would come in for an abortion). What I actually thought was, "you got yourself into this, now deal with it."

When a woman would call the clinic, I would try to make her feel that it was her decision, and that we were behind her, because women usually seek other women who agree with their decision.

• **Luhra Tivis:** A woman called on behalf of her daughter inquiring about the procedure. She also asked, "Has there ever been a live birth?" That question shocked me, because I had never considered it. So I asked my supervisor, Elena, about it. She told me, "Tell her that we have never had any live births in this clinic." Later, I discovered that that was a lie.

SOURCE: "Abortion, The Inside Story", a video from "The Pro-Life Action League", 1995. Translated and quoted by "Vida Humana Internacional" (Human Life International).

Statement of a Hispanic Ex-abortionist in the U.S.

• **Dr. José María Arrunategui**: I would perform abortions during the first trimester of a pregnancy. But there was one time when the patient was about 10 to 13 weeks into her pregnancy. I did what I usually would do and after dilating the cervix, as I was removing the tissue, one of the pieces fell to the floor and the nurse exclaimed, "Doctor, I think that is... is it a hand?". At first I didn't see what she was referring to, but then I took a closer look, and without a doubt it was a little hand that seemed to be imploring, "Please don't". Later that little hand made me admit that I was guilty. Up until that moment I had only seen a handful of tissue, but later, as I was developing my relationship with Christ, I realized that it was a beautifully designed hand.

SOURCE: Taken from the program "Speak Up for Life", a documentary broadcast aired January 18, 1997 on EWTN. the television network of Mother Angelica, in Alabama, U.S.A. The statement is from Dr. José Maria Arrunategui, from Peru.

Statement of a Former Abortionist in the U.S.

I told the members of my church that I had killed my own baby. I thought they could never forgive me. In my mind, abortion was the unpardonable sin.

When I finished speaking, I was received with love – and yes, forgiveness- into the arms of the people who lovingly rescued me from the abortion industry and who are now willing to help me see myself through the eyes of a God of love and forgiveness. I couldn't believe it, I cried uncontrollably.

At that moment, by means of the acceptance of His people, God cleansed me with His unconditional love. That night, I knew that the blood of Jesus shed for me on the cross covered me completely and forgave all of my sins. I was no longer the "Scarlet Lady", covered with the blood of over 35,000 aborted children, not even with the blood of my own child. Now the Scarlet Lady was covered with the blood of Jesus.

SOURCE: Statement of Carol Everett from Celebrate Life magazine (March-April 1996 issue). Carol Everett, former abortionist and owner of abortion clinics, is currently president of Life Network and author of "The Scarlet Lady".

Statement of a Former Abortionist in Hungary

I am a doctor who used to perform abortions. Now I have been converted and am pro-life. I am secretary of the "Obstetras por la Vida" (Obstetricians for Life) organization in Hungary. We try to foster an environment of true guilt free conscience for our colleagues, and establish obstetric and gynecology departments in our country so that abortion is not performed.

Now I recognize how the diabolical anti-life forces were at work through my activities. I killed because my conscience was dead. I regret that there was a time in my life when thought that one could be a good Catholic and still perform abortions. But how is that possible? A few years ago I went to confession, after having been away from the sacraments for about 20 years, and the priest asked me if I would be fired if I didn't perform abortions. I told him I would, and then he gave me absolution in the name of God and didn't say anything more.

I continued performing abortions for a while, until returned to confession one day. It was on Christmas night and I found a good priest, may God bless him. He told me clearly and firmly that I was living in a state of excommunication. Without that loving intervention from God, I never would have stopped the killing.

What am I talking about? With the existing secularism here in Hungary, it is necessary for clergy and laymen alike to be completely faithful to the teachings of the Church in order to develop a good conscience. Any variance in this matter will result in a false conscience, in a distorted vision in which we will never recognize what is wrong or, what sin is. So I tried to form my concept about what it meant to be pro-life, as a doctor and as a believer.

The life of every human being starts at the moment d fertilization, and physically continues until the moment of death. Human life is procreated to love and be loved, life means love. To be pro-life, then, is to do the things promote an absolute respect for life. It means saying, "no" to all birth control methods whose purpose is to destroy human life, to abortion, to fetal and embryonic experimentation, and to euthanasia. To be pro-life is to recognize that all sexuality and fertility are wonderful gifts that God has given us for the service of life and love. They can bring a balance to the nature of man, which consists of a soul and a body. We should practice chastity before marriage, and fidelity and natural family planning within marriage (when it is for the purpose of spacing out the births).

At the same time, to be pro-life is to expose deceitful philosophies and trends that lead our neighbor down a path of death, selfishness and secular humanism. In other words: a consumer mentality about life and love is based on a false concept of man that comes from the Father of Lies: the devil.

The activities that come from this two-fold purpose should be carried out in all the professions: politics, legislatures, education, medicine, all of which need to be organized in a highly professional manner. But the main purpose of all these activities is to lovingly and effectively come to the aid of any person who is suffering, like the Good Samaritan did. Pro-life is pro-love. And to be truly pro-love is to be pro-God. You, the leaders of the pro-life movement present here, belong to the group of the Good Samaritans, those who ran to Jerusalem to alert the people so they could get organized and protect their city from the robbers on the highway. All of you are that kind of people: pro-life, pro love and pro-God.

Thank you for your invaluable and encouraging example. Thanks to the Church for teaching the truth. Thank God for all of you.

SOURCE: Dr. András Szörényi presentation, at the World Pro-Life Summit in Rome. Dr. Szörényi is leader of the pro-life movement in Hungary.